The Murder of Sister Margaret Ann Pahl

Ana Benson

Published by Trellis Publishing, 2021.

While every precaution has been taken in the preparation of this book, the publisher assumes no responsibility for errors or omissions, or for damages resulting from the use of the information contained herein.

THE MURDER OF SISTER MARGARET ANN PAHL

First edition. July 2, 2021.

ISBN: 979-8224121557

Written by Ana Benson.

THE MURDER OF SISTER MARGARET ANN PAHL

ANA BENSON

Before the satanic panic of the mid-80s and the accusations of the sexual abuse within the institution, the Catholic Church managed to cover up a murder in Toledo, Ohio. It shouldn't come as a surprise because they were a very powerful organization back in the day and would do anything to save their reputation, including manipulation. The murder victim was a nun, and the only suspect – a priest.

Knowing how the public would react if this got out to the media, the higher-ups from the Catholic Church stopped the investigation completely, removing the accused from the area. However, it took a single letter from 2003 for this case to be re-examined in a new light. And after more than two decades later, the justice was finally served.

Margaret Ann Pahl's early life

Margaret Ann Pahl was born on April 6th, 1909 in a highly religious family. She wanted to become a nurse from an early age, so she studied medicine prior to her decision to become a nun. Margaret joined the Sisters of Mercy when she was only nineteen years old. The Sisters of Mercy is a well-known religious institute created in Ireland, but it quickly spread out throughout the globe. She put her medical knowledge to use and soon became a registered nurse, as well as a nun who dedicated her life to helping those in need.

As the time went by, Sister Margaret Ann Pahl continued her work at the Mercy Hospital in Toledo, Ohio. She was there to consult the younger members of the Sisters of Mercy, and show them the basics. Sister Margaret Ann Pahl was known for her strictness and perfectionism. She didn't hesitate to tell everyone what she really thinks and was very outspoken. Since Mercy Hospital had a chapel, Margaret did her best to keep it in order. She would wake up every morning at 05:00 AM, and start her duties. There were more than twenty nuns at the hospital, and all of them were there to learn from Sister Margaret Ann Pahl.

Besides the nuns, there were also two priests living at the hospital. Their names were Father Gerald Robinson and Father Jerome Swiatecki. They were there to take care of the sick patients and those who are terminally ill. However, Sister Margaret Ann Pahl wasn't keen on Father Gerald Robinson. The two of them quarreled a lot during the time they spent together working at the hospital. As a matter of fact, the majority of the staff, as well as the nuns were familiar with the fact that Margaret Ann Pahl disliked Father Robinson.

Gerald Robinson also came from a religious family, and his mother was the one who made her son become a clergyman. He was born in Toledo, Ohio and stayed in his hometown for the entirety of his life. His mother financed Gerald's religious schooling from an early age, and he entered the priesthood when he was twenty-six years old. Catholic Church decided to keep him in Toledo to work in a hospital alongside Sister Margaret Ann Pahl. Their personalities simply clashed because Robinson mostly kept to himself, and Sister Margaret thought that he wasn't doing a good job. But he was still loved by the parishioners because he was fluent in Polish and Toledo had a large Eastern European community. So when the two of them got into a fight on April 4th, 1980 because he cut off his sermon early, and Sister Margaret Ann Pahl felt like he owed the parishioners to see it until the end because tomorrow was the Easter Sunday, nobody found it strange or out of the ordinary.

The discovery of the body

It was April 5th, 1980 when one of the nuns opened the doors to the chapel in order to start the early preparations for the Easter Sunday. The hospital expected that the chapel will be completely filled because Easter Sunday is one of the biggest celebrations among Catholics. But as soon as she entered the room, the nun saw a shocking image in front of her. Margaret Ann Pahl's body was laying in the middle of the chapel.

The woman was stabbed, and it was clear that something violent has happened during the night. The nun ran outside in a state of panic. She was searching for the phone to call the authorities.

When the investigators arrived at the scene, they were appalled by the viciousness of the murder. The nun was first strangled from behind and then laid down on the floor, where the killer continued to inflict her stab wounds all over her body. The wounds were mostly around her face, on the neck, and torso. However, the killer took the altar cloth and placed it over Sister Margaret Ann's chest before they stabbed her. When the police lifted the cloth off her body, they noticed that the stabs formed an inverted cross. This was a clear indication they were dealing with someone deranged and insane. They weren't sure if the murder had anything to do with Satanism, but everything pointed in that direction. Sister Margaret Ann Pahl also had a bloody cross drawn on her forehead which suggested that the last rite ceremony was performed on her body. In the end, the examiners counted a total of thirty-one stab wounds on Sister Margaret Ann Pahl.

Another detail that was shocking to the investigators was the fact that Margaret Ann's skirt was pulled up, exposing her lower body. The killer also took off her underwear, leaving it around her ankles. However, they couldn't determine if the nun was sexually assaulted because the murder scene looked very clean. It left them wondering if everything was staged to make it appear like the woman was also raped before or after the murder. Since it was the early 1980s and the DNA technology was not fully developed, the investigators had troubles finding any physical evidence on Sister Margaret Ann, or around her body.

The initial investigation

Once they analyzed the scene, the detectives started interviewing everyone in the hospital at the time. They first talked to the nuns who were also deeply disturbed about everything that happened. The majority of them mentioned Father Gerald Robinson and his relationship with Sister Margaret Ann. There were obvious tensions between the two of them, and the nuns thought that he might be involved in a way. However, they weren't sure if he was the killer because he was very withdrawn and quiet. It was hard to imagine that he could hurt anyone.

The entire hospital was searched because the investigators believed that the perpetrator was still there, hiding in plain sight. They went into each room occupied by the nuns and the priests. The detectives found an interesting item in Father Gerald Robinson's accommodation. It was a letter opener that resembled a small dagger. The blade could have been the one which was used to inflict the wounds found on Sister Margaret Ann Pahl's body. Knowing that the two of them argued on the day before the murder, the detectives were fairly certain that they had their suspect. But the letter opener was completely clean, just like the murder scene, and there were no visible traces of blood on it. However, a further analysis showed that there was some DNA material at the bottom of the blade. Unfortunately, it wasn't enough to run the full test in order to determine if it belonged to the murder victim or the killer.

Things were moving fast at the chapel, and the funeral for Sister Margaret Ann Pahl was held on April 8th, 1980. Since Margaret Ann didn't have many relatives in the area, the attendees were the nuns and priests from the hospital. Father Gerald Robinson wasn't officially accused of the killing, and he was not taken into the custody. He was allowed to lead the service for the murdered woman. Father Swiatecki was also there, and he also added a couple of sentences during the funeral.

With only one possible suspect, the police brought Father Gerald Robinson to the police station two weeks after the crime occurred. They wanted to conduct an official interview and hear what he had to say about the night when Sister Margaret Ann was killed. However, before the interview actually started, a monsignor appeared in the police station, and he led Father Robinson out. Soon enough, Father Robinson was transferred from the Mercy Hospital in order to become a pastor. He stayed in the area and was in charge of three parishes in Toledo. He continued to live and work like nothing happened. It was obvious to the detectives who were on this case that something was wrong. But they had no physical evidence that could connect the priest with the murder. And with that, the murder of Sister Margaret Ann Pahl became a cold case.

The cover-ups weren't unusual for the Catholic Church back in the days. They were still very powerful in the 1980s and were capable of hiding their own scandals. If something bad happened within the church, the high-ranking clergymen would intervene almost immediately. They had a developed system that would hide the crimes from the authorities. So the fact that they moved Father Robinson to a different parish wasn't strange at all. This was the best way to conceal the crime and influence the investigators to stop digging deeper. But the 1990s changed everything because the public became familiar with the sexual abuse within the church itself. The witnesses started coming forward, and soon enough, the investigators throughout the United States had more evidence about cold cases that were dormant for decades.

A new witness

The files about the murder of Sister Margaret Ann Pahl laid untouched for a total of twenty-three years. With no new leads or witnesses, the investigators were sure that the case will remain unsolved. It seemed like nobody was willing to talk. But everything changed in 2003 when one witness came forward. As previously mentioned, many women and children started speaking with the authorities about the abuse they suffered from the Catholic priests. An anonymous female sent a letter to Toledo Police Department in 2003. In it, she claimed that she went through a process of recovering her own memories and that she discovered she was a part of the satanic rituals performed by the Catholic priests when she was just a young girl. Since the experience was highly traumatic, her own mind managed to conceal it.

Probably the most interesting part of that letter was that she identified one of the priests involved in the satanic rituals. His name was Father Gerald Robinson. The detectives in Toledo knew the man well. They remembered he was the prime suspect in the murder of Sister Margaret Ann Pahl. The details of that case were very similar to the satanic rituals. After all, the nun was found with the stab wounds that formed an inverted cross. The anonymous woman who sent the letter to the police also mentioned that the priests involved in these rituals performed human sacrifice. Taking everything into the consideration, the investigators decided to open up the case once again in hopes that they missed something which could connect Father Gerald Robinson to the killing of Sister Margaret Ann Pahl.

The woman who sent the letter used the name Survivor Doe to file a civil lawsuit. She claimed that Father Gerald Robinson sexually abused her during the satanic rituals he performed. Survivor Doe said that there were other adults present in the room and she urged them to come out and testify on her behalf. She was unable to identify them on her own because they were wearing nun uniforms and their faces have been covered. Unfortunately, the case itself went nowhere due to the lack of evidence. It was finally dismissed in 2011 and Father Gerald Robinson wasn't charged with the sexual abuse of a minor. But Toledo Police Department started working hard on the case as soon as they received Survivor Doe's letter. New detectives were examining the physical evidence, and they had the technology that would give them better answers.

The re-opening of the case

The arrival of Survivor Doe's letter encouraged the investigators to re-examine the evidence that was collected at the crime scene. This also included the letter opener previously owned by Father Gerald Robinson. The letter opener looked like a small sword or a dagger. Even though the detectives who worked on the case in 1980 suspected that it might be the murder weapon, they never conducted a thorough examination. Toledo Police Department asked for the nun's body to be exhumed, and they sent it to the forensic unit alongside with the letter opener. They determined that one of the facial wounds was very likely inflicted with the letter opener because the blade was an almost perfect fit. However, they couldn't say that the blade was indeed the murder weapon.

After going through the interviews which were conducted immediately after the murder, the detectives noticed that several nuns who were working with Sister Margaret Ann Pahl mentioned that the woman always had a pair of scissors with her. They weren't found in her possession, or anywhere near the murder scene, which led the investigators to believe that the scissors might have been the murder weapon all along. Someone clearly picked them up and hid them from the police. They tested the stab wounds on Sister Margaret Ann's exhumed body and confirmed that scissors might have been the murder weapon as well.

Finally, the forensic unit took the swabs from underneath Sister Margaret Ann's fingernails, as well as from the inside of her underwear. The DNA technology wasn't as advanced in the 1980s but now they could test it in order to find the suspect. Sure enough, the swabs revealed that there was a presence of a male DNA under the nails and in her underwear. But it wasn't a match to Father Gerald Robinson. It belonged to a second person which led the investigators to suspect that there was more than one killer present at the chapel that night.

Since the investigators already had a list of people who were interviewed by the police back in 1980, they decided it might be time to talk to then again. They spoke with everyone they could locate and this led to the discovery of the brand new evidence which wasn't documented more than two decades ago. The police now had witnesses that were able to place Father Gerald Robinson near the crime scene around the time of the murder. It is still unclear why the witnesses failed to mention this detail during the initial investigation, but this allowed the detectives to start building the case against Father Robinson. He was near the chapel when Sister Margaret Ann Pahl was murdered and was in possession of the possible murder weapon.

Then they proceeded to interview Father Robinson himself who willingly went to the police station and gave them his own recollection of the murder. Father Robinson said that he was taking a shower when a nun entered his room in order to inform him that Sister Margaret was found dead in the chapel. He dressed in a hurry and went to the crime scene to see what was happening. When questioned about the murder back in 1980, Father Robinson said something very curious to the investigators. He told them that a man confessed to him that he murdered Sister Margaret Ann, but the priest had no authority to disclose the man's name. However, when asked to confirm this statement in 2004, Father Robinson claimed that he made the story up. Surely, they weren't able to produce a good motive for the murder, but the detectives hoped that Father Robinson would finally start telling the truth about the events that occurred on the night before the Easter Sunday back in 1980.

The arrest and the trial

On April 23rd, 2004 the investigators Tom Ross and Sargent Steve Forrester arrested Father Gerald Robinson for the murder of Sister Margaret Ann Pahl. They picked him up at his home in Toledo, Ohio.

He was still working as a priest at the time of his arrest. He pleaded not guilty on May 7th, 2004. Father Robinson was set to wait for the trial out of the jail because his family managed to pay a $400,000 bond. Also, the church placed him on leave which meant that he was not allowed to perform any religious ceremonies during this time. The accusations were shocking to some of the parishioners who knew Father Gerald Robinson for years. As a matter of fact, he gathered a huge following who supported the claims of his innocence. One parishioner called Jack Sparagowski started collecting money that would pay off the defense fees for Father Robinson. He raised a total of $12,000. When asked why he believed in Father Robinson's innocence, Sparagowski told the following: *"For someone to commit murder, you have to have a violent streak. I've never heard Father raise his voice or show any expression of anger. The whole thing seems so bizarre."*

The investigators working on this cold case were not sure if they should mention the satanic part of the murder. Dave Davison who was the first police officer on the scene stood firm with his beliefs that the whole ritualistic setup of the murder was actually another cover-up which was supposed to steer the investigation into a wrong direction. Prior to the trial, Ross and Forrester invited Dawn Perlmutter who is an expert in ritualistic killings, to hear her own take on the murder. Having in mind that Survivor Doe spoke about satanic rituals in her letter, the prosecution was willing to mention this part during the trial. However, Perlmutter advised them to avoid the narrative because the public is not eager to accept that these things actually do happen and that they might have a hard time convincing the jury.

The trial began on April 17th, 2006 in a Lucas County courtroom. The judge was Thomas Osowik, and he handled numerous high-profile cases in Toledo, Ohio. The media covered the trial thoroughly, and it quickly became one of the most interesting events in Ohio that year. However, there was also some backlash from the public, namely the members of the community who believed that the police was once again covering up the grisly details of the sexual abuse in the Catholic Church. Claudia Vercelloti who is a director of Survivors Network of those Abused by Priests in Toledo, criticized the authorities for focusing their investigation on the murder only. She was positive that there was more to it, and that the sexual abuse described in Survivor Doe's letter needed to be tied in with the killing as well. After all, Survivor Doe named Father Gerald Robinson as one of the abusers. Vercelloti said the following: *"We know this is a trial about murder, but the cover-up can't be ignored."*

Dean Mandros was appointed as the lead prosecutor, and Chris Anderson was chosen as a part of the team. Both of them were very successful in the past and confident that they could win this case as well, even though they only had circumstantial evidence. Father Robinson found excellent defense layers - Alan Konop and John Thebes. The trial began after the jury selection, and the first to testify was Sister Phyllis Ann Gerold. She was the one who saw Father Gerald Robinson near the scene of the crime at the time the murder was committed. Sister Gerold confirmed that Father Robinson was not in his room and that he was on the floor where the chapel was located.

Even though the prosecution was advised not to mention the ritualistic murders during the trial, they invited Father Jeffrey Grob as one of their witnesses. Father Grob is an expert when it comes to analyzing different rituals. While he avoided connecting the murder to Satanism, he did mention that a priest would have enough knowledge to stage the murder scene and make it appear like a ritual was performed on the body of the victim. He wasn't able to confirm that Sister Margaret Ann Pahl was killed during the ritual itself, but Father Grob said that an inverted cross was a very common symbol in Satanism.

The prosecution managed to recruit a famous forensic investigator Dr. Henry Lee who was a part of several prominent cases including the murder of JonBenet Ramsey and the O.J. Simpson trial. Dr. Henry

Lee was there to give his assessment of the possible murder weapon, as well as to determine if the crime scene was staged. While he confirmed that the letter opener which was found in Father Robinson's possession could have been the blade which was used to kill Sister Margaret Ann Pahl, he was uncertain about the imprints on the altar cloth. One bloody trace was very similar to the decorations found on the handle of the letter opener. Dr. Henry Lee could not dismiss the claims that the murder scene was staged in order to look like a sexual assault, as well as a satanic ritual.

The defense called Dr. Kathy Reichs, a well-known forensic anthropologist to give her own evaluations of the wounds found on Sister Margaret Ann Pahl's exhumed body. Dr. Reichs said that the findings were inconclusive and she suspected that another weapon was used to kill Sister Pahl. However, she couldn't rule out the possibility either. Dr. Reichs mentioned that the scissors owned by Sister Margaret Ann Pahl were a more believable murder weapon. She came to this conclusion after examining the images of the stab wounds provided to her by the defense.

Father Gerald Robinson stayed silent during the trial. He never spoke to anyone and refused to testify on his behalf. His defense lawyers argued that the prosecution had no physical evidence tying their defendant to the murder. Everything they presented was circumstantial, including the letter opener. Not to forget that an unknown male DNA was discovered at the scene as well. The defense also stated that Father Robinson didn't have any motive for the murder which sparked a heated discussion about the fact that Father Robinson argued with Sister Pahl one day before the killing.

The verdict and aftermath

The jury retreated to discuss the case on May 11th, 2006. It took them only six hours of deliberation to reach the verdict. Father

Robinson sat in the courtroom, wearing his clerical collar, looking calm and composed. The jury found him guilty of the murder of Sister Margaret Ann Pahl. The judge sentenced him to fifteen years to life, with the possibility of a parole after ten and a half years. Father Robinson refused to comment on the ruling, not breaking his silence throughout the whole procedure. He was escorted to Lucas County jail.

As the prosecution exited the courtroom, they were cheered by the people waiting for the sentencing. Dean Mandros, the lead prosecutor made a comment immediately after leaving the court in which he said: *"I don't see it as a reason to celebrate. We're dealing with a homicide case. We're trying to hold the person responsible accountable. We didn't go back in the office and high-five each other."* Mandros also mentioned that he was certain Father Robinson murdered Sister Margaret Ann Pahl in a fit of blind rage. When asked about the ritualistic part of the murder, he dismissed it. Instead, Mandros said: *"Perhaps the most common scenario there is for a homicide: A man got very angry at a woman and the woman died. The only thing different is that the man wore a white collar and the woman wore a habit."*

Father Gerald Robinson suffered a heart attack in May of 2014. He died on July 4th, 2014 in Franklin Medical Center in Columbus, Ohio where he was imprisoned. Father Robinson became a first known Catholic priest in the United States who was found guilty of murdering a nun.

GOD TOLD ME TO: THE TRUE STORY OF GWEN HENDRICKS

14

PAULA HEARST

Gwen Gillespie Hendricks was born into a Navy family in Memphis, Tennessee in 1955.

Her father was a naval officer while her mother was a housewife. Like most military families, they moved often from station to station, according to her father's assignment. Growing up in a devoutly Catholic home and Gwen would embrace the religion with fervor.

Gwen dressed with modesty, wearing button down shirts and minimal make-up. She fostered a nerd look, with wire-rimmed glasses and short hair.

Carrying on the family's military tradition, she joined the Air Force at the age of twenty-five. It was there she would meet Jim Hendricks, twenty-four, who was her instructor.

Jim Hendricks was a tall, strapping Air Force sergeant with an air of authority. He had an easy smile and Gwen found him easy on the eyes.

"Well, it was kind of instant attraction," Gwen recalled. "There was a bit of lust there as he's a very tall, handsome man. The Air Force can tell you that you can't date but they can't tell you who to marry so I went to the Jag office and asked if I could marry my STA and they said 'yes.'"

The two were married in 1980. Jim had a five year old daughter, Season Hendricks, from a previous relationship. In 1982, they would have a son, Ben.

Because of their career choice, the couple spent a lot of time apart during the early years of their marriage. Jim was stationed at Wake Island while Gwen was assigned to Eglin Air Force Base in Florida.

The couple would be reunited in 1986 as Jim was assigned to the Air Force Academy in Colorado Springs. Gwen would not re-enlist in the Air Force, instead taking a job with the Internal Revenue Service.

The couple spent three years in Colorado before Jim would be transferred to Guam in August of 1989. He took the the entire family with him to the island.

"I figured we had a pretty normal family," Season said. "Until we moved to Guam. Things started to change. She (Gwen) would pick fights. She was jealous of the time my Dad and I would spend together."

"She (Gwen) had a different life in mind for herself," forensic psychologist Joyce Smith said. "She was used to having her own money. So when they moved to Guam there was little to do and less money to do it with."

Gwen and the children moved back to the United States, returning to Colorado and leaving Jim in Guam.

She would buy a home in Littleton and once again start working for the IRS. She then joined the junior Chamber of Commerce where she met Terry Knaack and a woman named Rochelle.

"Rochelle was into tarot cards," Gwen said. "And Terry was into new age occultism. My religion, my faith was still very meaningful to me. I wanted to do Bible study with them to get them out of what I considered witchcraft. Rochelle said she wouldn't go to Bible study with me unless I did the cards with her and the same with Terry. So I think I opened up the door to hell. Right after I started, everything went wrong."

During this time, Gwen began to experience health issues. She suffered from dizzy spells and nausea.

Her personality shifted as well, changing from being even-tempered to easily agitated and manic. With her health and ability to focus effected, Gwen stepped down from her revenue collector position to tax examiner.

"Could the illness have played a part in her deciding to kill her husband?" Smith asked. "Maybe. But Gwen was really steeped into religion and sounded like she embraced some of the more fringe elements of Christianity. She truly believed that occultism was a form of witchcraft and that those things could do her harm. So when she suffered from her illness she erroneously attributed it to her dabbling in the occult. She was a woman who preferred supernatural explanations to rational thought."

Gwen also started to grow deeper into debt, buying expensive gifts for friends.

In the fall of 1990, Gwen hired Terry Knaack to help remodel the Littleton home. A few months later, Knaack moved into the couple's basement with the rationale being he would be able to help with the mortgage. With the husband away and a man in the home, Gwen began to fantasize about Terry and starting over with him.

"Terry would talk a lot about wanting to having a ranch for children with special needs," Gwen recalled. "And I started having delusions that he and I would start this ranch together for the children."

"She entered into a fantasy world," Smith said. "She began imagining a life with this other man, having delusions of grandeur of what they would do together. He became her willing accomplice in her dreams, since her own husband was absent because of military duty. So an alternate universe with Terry Knaack became her obsession. What probably started as harmless day dreams soon grew into something sinister."

"I also believe that Gwen had more than a little bit of a Messiah complex. She had this compulsion to save people and it manifested in doling out gifts and handouts to people who she felt were in need. She had this secret life and kept things from Jim who was away on military assignment. Those secrets involved getting into credit card debt."

By January of 1991, Gwen began telling friends that she was having premonitions of Jim dying in a plane crash.

"I had this really bad dream over and over again," Gwen recalled. "Where Jim had died in a plane crash. I was thinking, well after Jim died that I would marry Terry and we'd start this ranch but of course Terry didn't know anything about because it was all in my head."

Gwen then began hearing voices.

"They (the voices) wanted me to sacrifice what was most dear in my life," Gwen recalled. "I remember thinking that I have to answer these voices because this is coming from God. You know, I've got to sacrifice what I loved the most and that was Jim."

Gwen kept a journal where she logged the "premonitions" of her husband's death. She titled the journal "The Courage to Will and Persevere," She described the voices that she heard and believed that God had told her to kill Jim.

"She experienced what we call 'command hallucinations,'" said Smith. "These are sometimes coupled with someone's value system, in this case, it was Gwen's religion. Gwen believed that she should obey God and believed that the voices that she heard were, in fact, coming from God. So this could go bad real quick if those voices told her to do damage to someone."

"She was past the breaking point, a delusional schizophrenic that was not diagnosed. When she confided with friends it was probably with people who shared her same point of view, people who believed in visions, messages from God and premonitions. Gwen was a soft-spoken woman and even if someone thought she was crazy they would not think she would be capable of taking a gun and blowing someone's brains out. She didn't have that violent vibe."

But behind closed doors, Gwen would deal with problems or difficulties in a haphazard fashion. She would often open up the Bible and believed that whatever random verse she came upon was a direct message from God.

"I reread Psalm 90 quite a few times before a small voice said, 'Keep reading, keep reading.'" Gwen wrote in her journal. "After reading the first page of stanzas, I knew I would be protected from the car bombs, the knifings, the guns, the contracts and all the other evil I had seen connected with busting the pornographers and pimps. Those mafia guys play rough, but somehow they just won't be able to get me. Then I turned the page to continue reading. It felt like a giant fist had slammed into my heart. I literally could not breath [sic]. I burst into sobs and sunk to the floor. I cried for Jim because he really was going to die."

Gwen began to prepare for Jim's death, taking out a $300,000 life insurance policy on her husband payable on his death.

She then visited a local banker, informing him that she would be soon be receiving proceeds from insurance claim. Gwen was told that she would not be able to use the money as long as Jim was alive. She then forged a doctor's note which alleged that she had multiple sclerosis. She submitted this note to the Red Cross along with a letter stating that they should be responsible for being her husband back from Guam.

Gwen did not want the proceeds from the insurance for her own material gain. She believed that she could use the proceeds from his life insurance to establish the "James

Hendricks Foundation" to aid victims of mafia produced pornography.

"She became obsessed with pornographers," Smith said. "Like most people with Messiah Complexes, she chose an ill of society and focused on that, believing that she was a chosen vessel to help eradicate the 'sin'. In her deluded mind, she needed this money to accommodate God's will to establish this ranch wherein she would save victims of pornography. The only way she could attain this goal would be to kill Jim and take the life insurance proceeds."

"I was very desperate to have him (Jim) back," Gwen said. "I felt like I was at my limit and not really realizing that I actually was really having a breakdown."

With her husband not even dead yet, Gwen began purchasing clothes for herself and the children to wear for his funeral.

She bought silk flowers and boxes of Kleenex for mourning friends and family.

Gwen also increased the amount of Jim's life insurance from $300,000 to $1,000,000.

True to her premonition, she bought a wedding dress for herself and put a wedding ring on layaway for Knaack.

Gwen would ask God to speak to her directly and "guide her hand" as she thumbed through her Bible. When she got to a passage, she would believe that was what God wanted her to study."

"For the first reading, only the last sentence made sense," *Gwen wrote. "I had asked if what I felt about Jim's death was* *real. He said yes.*

God can even speak through the dictionary!

After reading the first page of stanzas, I knew I would be *protected from car bombs, the knifings, the guns, the contracts* *and all the other evil I had seen connected with busting* *pornographers and pimps. Those Mafia guys play rough, but* *somehow they just won't be able to get me."*

"You can see her delusions of grandeur in her journal writings," Smith said. "She had all of the symptoms of a delusional narcissist, truly believing that God made her as the 'Chosen One.'"

Gwen would write that she had a two-way conversation with God about creating the ranch.

"'Oh, so the ranch is in Douglas county near to the Springs *so my family will be protected from the mafia guys' Then I knew* *in Denver, I'm Gwen Hendricks. In the Springs, I'm Gwen* *Knaack. I had thought the clinic would carry the name of the* *ranch, but with this new insight, I knew that for safety sake,* *everything had to be kept separate."*

She continued to have health issues as well, as the nausea and attacks of dizziness still had not subsided. Physicians could not determine the cause of her illness. She was eventually diagnosed with Ménière's disease, an ailment that causes vertigo and a fluctuating hearing loss. She had a micro-shunt placed into her ear which only helped relieve the pain she was experiencing.

Her mental health, however, continued to deteriorate.

Jim would return to Colorado for good in May of 1991. It would not be a well-received reunion, however, as the couple fought over everything specifically the living arrangements of Knaack. Jim promptly kicked the boarder out of the home.

He then took control of the finances as he discovered that Gwen had maxed out the credit cards.

"My brother said that she had apparently taken several other credit cards and had maxed them out to the limit," recalled Steve Hendricks, Jim's brother. "And he was furious with her at that point. He did confide in me that he was thinking about leaving Gwen."

Jim would take away all of Gwen's credit cards and this made her extremely angry.

"He took away her power," Smith said. "She got an ego boost by buying expensive gifts for friends and helping out women that she thought were in need. When Jim took that away, she saw him as someone who needed to be eliminated."

Divorce seemed imminent but Gwen seemed immune to it all in her journal writings.

"The funeral, the ranch school, children, the foundation, always being pushed forward," she wrote. *"I have to do what I have to do, too. But just for now I'm going to take one day at a time. I'm hoping I don't get too compulsed to do anything more for at least this coming week. I need to rest.*

Perhaps I should start by explaining the little voice. It's my voice, but not me. It comes from somewhere inside, and if I don't listen to it, act on it, it becomes a compulsion. If I don't listen and act on the compulsion, it grows stronger and stronger until it dominates all aspects of my life. I learned long ago to listen and do what I'm told. Things work out when I do, and when I don't, things get real miserable...Yes, my little voice is the way God reaches me with the Holy Spirit."

With Jim now home on a permanent basis, The voices in her head grew louder. They began to speak with more urgency in telling her that she had to kill her husband.

"True to her religious background, she did not interpret auditory hallucinations as a sign of mental illness," Smith said. "Gwen was the kind of woman who took the stories in the Bible literally, seeing herself as a modern day Abraham who heard voices from God. You hear it in the way she describes the voices in her head telling her to sacrifice her husband in the same way the Bible speaks of God telling Abraham to sacrifice his son Isaac."

"I said 'Lord I surrender to you,'" Gwen recalled. "I'm hearing voices from God and this is what God wants and I have to get this from God and if this is what God wants then I have to give it to him. So I went out and I bought a gun"

"The voices in her head told her it was time," Smith said. "And true to her value system, she had to obey. For her religion was not a therapeutic aid because of the way she had viewed it. Her God was a vengeful one, a violent one."

On Friday, August 17th, 1991 Gwen drove to Peterson Air Force Base to meet with her husband, a 75 mile drive, to bring him a change of clothes.

"Jim was working late and he asked me to bring him something to eat." Gwen said.

She had informed police that Jim was working all night to prepare for an inspection but changed his mind.

Gwen wrote in her journal about the incident.

When Jim called to say he was on his way home, I went into shock. I knew the time was at hand. I knew I wasn't really ready. I screamed and cried and raged. Then I asked again, if he was meant to die or was I just suckered into some kind of head game. Benjamin's daddy died. I cried myself to sleep that night. I thought what was I supposed to do with two husbands. God has the oddest sense of humor."

"She told me that she was gonna make a nice little picnic for them," Gwen's step-daughter Season recalled. "They were going to make a night of it and that she wanted him to feel good for his inspection."

Gwen left the home and dropped off both Season and son Ben with a friend. When Gwen arrived at the Air Force base, however, she stated that Jim told her that he was heading home. She maintained that the two then went back home in separate cars.

"His truck was in the lead," Gwen said. "I was in the car behind. I remember being so tired, I told him I can't go on anymore. I just want a quick nap and let's get in the back of the truck."

She said that they traveled in separate cars but she became tired and slept through the night at a rest stop along Interstate 25.

Police, however, believed that Gwen lured Jim to an abandoned stretch of highway with the promise of sex.

The two met at the side of the road and Gwen hesitated when thinking of pulling out the gun. She wanted her husband to go peacefully.

"I took the gun out from underneath the seat of the car," Gwen said. "I got into the truck and laid next to him and when I could feel that he was deeply sleeping that's when I shot him."

Gwen would shoot Jim six times.

"It was like I was outside of myself," Gwen said. "Looking and watching what I was doing. I felt very numb, very cold, like I was on auto-pilot. I got back into my car and I took apart the gun and I was just throwing the parts out the window and just driving around, just in a fog, not knowing what I was doing, where I was going. I stopped at a roadside rest stop. Fell asleep. When I woke up and I didn't know everything that happened."

When Gwen arrived back home that Saturday she began making calls to the police, stating that her husband was missing.

On Monday morning, she called Jim's supervisor who sent out two officers to search for him.

One of his co-workers would find his pickup truck on the side of Highway 83 in Douglas County. His body had been placed in the camper shell in back of his truck.

He had been shot six times in the chest and neck with a small caliber handgun.

Gwen would become the primary suspect.

Police noted that she hardly showed any emotion when they informed her of her husband's death.

"Her state of mind was that of a wife with a missing husband," one of the deputies recalled. "When she was telling a story, she couldn't stick with the same story. And that's a clue, obviously, to law enforcement."

Gwen would then break the news to Jim's daughter, Season.

"Gwen said they found him by the side of the road in his car," Season said. "And that he had been murdered. I don't remember her crying. It was the worst moment of my life."

Terry Knaack would be helpful in the case against Gwen. She had been secretly in love with him and given him her diary. He read through her writings and promptly delivered the diary to the Douglas County Sheriff's Department. The sheriffs then instructed him to call Gwen while they would listen in.

Gwen would tell Knaack that she didn't kill Jim but that she wanted to die. Then Douglas County Sheriff's Department Kim Castellano's intuition told her something was wrong. The Hendricks had two pre-teens, a boy and a girl and the boy was never around during questioning.

Castellano believed that Gwen had a problem with males. With one of the male investigators, an Air Force official, by her side, Castellano went back to talk to Gwen.

Once again, the boy was not there. Gwen was overly polite to Castellano, asking her if she wanted anything to eat and jumping up to fix her something before she could answer.

Gwen would totally ignored the male detective.

Castellano used this knowledge to her advantage and befriended Gwen, sensing that the delusional woman would be much more forthcoming with a female officer than a male.

Gwen began trusting her enough that she asked for Castellano's help in balancing her check book. The detective then saw that Hendricks had recently taken out several insurance policies that would be hers when her husband died.

The investigators then used a technique police refer to as the "midnight confession." Castellano and the Air Force official went over to the Hendricks house at eleven at night, waking Gwen up.

Questioning her in the family room, Gwen continued to deny her involvement in her husband's killing. Castellano and her partner then took turns reading from Gwen's journal, tightening the screws on her denial. They also saw Jim's watch on the counter.

Castellano then told her to get dressed and that she was being taken in.

Gwen finally cracked. She curled into a fetal position and confessed.

"Two stories that night—the story of the rest area and the story of Highway 83," she sobbed.

Gwen would go on to describe the highway story.

"There is blood everywhere, I can see it everywhere," she said. "It's terrible. My mind won't let me remember. I don't know if I shot him or not. I don't know what's real anymore."

Gwen was then taken to a local hospital where she stayed for two days for a mental health evaluation. She was arrested upon release and charged with her husband's murder.

After undergoing another mental health examination, Gwen was deemed delusional but understood the charges being levied against her.

Because of this, she was found fit to stand trial.

In court, however, Gwen continued to state that she didn't kill her husband. She said that the body found at the crime scene was not Jim's.

"There was the obvious choice for her attorneys to declare her insane," Smith said. "She had one hell of an imagination and could make things up on the fly. She said during the trial that she became completely convinced that her husband was still alive, going into full blown denial. 'He's still alive, he's out there somewhere and you have to find him', she would say. She was completely delusional."

Her first attorney, Lloyd Boyer, stated that it was physically impossible for Gwen to have murdered Jim Hendricks.

"The lack of gunshot residue inside the Capitol (Jim's car) vehicle," Boyer said. "Indicated that the murder had not occurred in the vehicle. Mr. Hendricks was quite a bit larger than Gwen and she was small, not especially strong and could not have moved the victim into the vehicle."

The investigators failed to produce the gun that Gwen used but the prosecution had another tool at its disposal.

The first link was Jim's watch that they found in Gwen's possession, which showed that she had tampered with the crime scene. The prosecution showed how she was going to use the money from the insurance policies and start a "home for troubled people" that would be near the spot where she killed her husband.

The jury found her guilty of first-degree murder and Hendricks was sentenced to life in prison.

"I just kept my faith that Jim would come rescue me and I would be set free from prison," Gwen said. "Of course, that never happened."

Inside the prison, physicians deemed her to be mentally unfit to be included with the general population and transferred her to the psychiatric unit.

"They got me on anti-psychotics," Gwen said. "And anti-depressants but it wasn't until 1997 that I started having memories of what had happened. At first, it was like just pictures and they hit me like bricks, you know. I killed a great husband and Dad. I robbed Season and Ben of their father. I felt lower than dirt."

She did have help, however, as some legal advocates filed briefs on her behalf, claiming that she had been insane at the time of her trial.

In September of 2000, the Supreme Court of Colorado overturned Gwen's conviction and ordered a new trial.

In April of 2001, a judge ruled that Gwen was not guilty by reason of insanity.

The trial lasted ten minutes.

"She came to terms with what she had done," Smith said. "She had stopped protesting, stop denying and admitted to what she had done."

Gwen was then remanded to a psychiatric care facility in Colorado. She then decided to change her name to "Emi Masai".

"When I lost Jim," Gwen said. "I also lost my children. I longed to be a wife and mother again. I redefined myself as married to Christ and being a mother to all the people I meet."

"By renaming herself she thought that she could obtain a new identity," Smith said. "It was a way of divorcing herself from her past transgressions."

Gwen went through four years of psychiatric treatment where the physicians determined that she was no longer a threat to society. She was released to a residential program where she now helps the needy at Mercy Ministries.

She continues to take her anti-psychotic medication.

"I never want to slip back into mental illness again," Gwen said. "I literally thank God every morning I open my medicine cabinet. I've always said justice wasn't done. Justice in this case would have been my execution. A life for a life. But it's not about fairness. It's about recognizing mental illness and knowing that you're not responsible for what you are doing when you're psychotic."

Gwen has had minimal contact with both her son and step-daughter since she committed the murder of their father.

"I long to see them but they let it be known through family channels that they don't want to see me," Gwen said. "So I respect that."

"I'm really glad that Gwen has helped herself enough to admit what she's done," Season said. "And I hope there never is a time where it gets easy for her to look in the mirror. Because there's never a time where it's easy to be without our Dad."

"I wish I could take it back," Gwen said. "Be a good wife and Mom again. I can't turn the clock back. So all I can do is give them my deepest apology and ask them to forgive me."

ARTHUR GARY BISHOP

BOB JANSEN

Arthur Gary Bishop—also known as Roger Downs and Lynn Jones—was a child molester/serial killer who sexually abused and murdered five young boys near Salt Lake City, Utah, between 1979 and 1983; at the height of serial killing in the United States. His preferred method of murder was either drowning or beating his helpless victims with a hammer. He was ultimately executed on 9 June 1988 by lethal injection after voluntary waiving any appeal claims.

Early Life

Arthur Gary Bishop was born on 29 September 1952 in Hinckley, Utah, a very small desert town with fewer than 700 residents that lies 100 miles southwest of Salt Lake City in Millard County. The eldest of six brothers, Bishop was raised by his parents as a devout Mormon and excelled in school, earning honor roll status, as well as becoming an Eagle Scout. Despite defense attorneys describing Bishop as a "lonely, frightened child" during his trial, there was no evidence to support said claim. In actuality, he appeared to be a model son and devout Mormon and the specter of abuse never came into public discourse.

School classmates remembered Bishop as "a geek, rarely if ever finding someone who would accept the rare offer of a date." His election as business manager for the high school student council failed to improve his popularity and classmates, again, said that voting a nerd to student council was "a tradition" and "a joke to humble the social elite during the coming year."

Nevertheless, Bishop's younger brother Douglas, four years his junior, idolized his big brother. So much, in fact, that Douglas was arrested and convicted of molesting and sexually assaulting 26 boys between five and 17 years of age from 1976 to 1983 outside of Provo, Utah. He is currently serving four terms of five-years-to-life and, interestingly, the brothers were arrested within three days of each other; however, at the time Douglas did not know where his brother was or what he had done. Despite being diagnosed as a homosexual pedophile himself, Douglas maintained that neither Arthur nor Douglas suffered any sexual abuse as children.

Upon graduating from high school in 1969, Bishop served as a missionary for the Church of Jesus Christ of the Latter Day Saints in the Philippines when he was 19 years of age. Bishop then graduated from Steven-Henager College—a business school that guarantees its students with "fast-track, career specific education"—with honors with a major in accounting and appeared to be following a stable and devout path to success.

However, despite Bishop's seeming normalcy, he possessed a darker side that nobody could have ever guessed by his overt success. He was addicted to and enthralled by child pornography and cultivated and nurtured fantasies which elaborated upon the images with which he was so enamored. It is impossible to ascertain when Bishop crossed that line from his morbid daydreams into becoming an active pedophile; however, experts surmise that a year after his excommunication he finally succumbed to the evil within him.

In February 1978, Bishop was convicted of embezzling nearly $9,000 from a used car dealership where he had been employed as a bookkeeper and, based upon his alleged repentance whether genuine or not, received a five-year suspended sentence on his promise of restitution; however, instead of returning the money he, instead, disappeared. A warrant for his arrest was subsequently issued. His failure to surrender caused the Mormon Church to excommunicate him in October 1978. When Bishop disappeared, he ended all communication with his family and friends, moved to another city, and reemerged as Lynn E. Jones and, later, Roger W. Downs.

By October of that same year he took on the alias of Roger Downs in Salt Lake City proper. He joined the Big Brother program to spend time with disadvantaged youth and his charisma and pseudo-father persona attracted numerous children who he lured into spending time with him at his home or joining him on camping trips; thus potentially providing him victims. At one point, spokespeople for the Big Brother/ Big Sister organization admitted receiving tips that a Mr. Downs had molested at least two children while working with them; however, neither of the victims was Bishop's "little brother." Allegedly, police were notified but did nothing with the information.

The Crimes

Alonzo Daniels, 4

The first young boy to disappear was four-year-old Alonzo Daniels, reported missing on 14 October 1979 from his Salt Lake City apartment complex. His worried mother enlisted the help of relatives and friends to search their complex and neighborhood but the young boy was never found. When police started conducting door-to-door searches they first talked to neighbor Roger Downs as his apartment was across the hall from where Daniels and his mother lived. Bishop answered the police's routine questions and denied having any knowledge of the location of the boy. At this point, unbeknownst to the police and his mother the child was already dead.

Bishop had lured Daniels to his home with the promise of candy. He attempted to undress and fondle the young boy in his living room but when the child began to cry and threatened to tell his mother Bishop struck him with a hammer. This did not stop the boy's sobbing so Bishop carried him into the bathroom and drowned him in the tub. When the child was dead Bishop stuffed him into a large cardboard box and took it out to his car; walking right past Daniels' mother who was in the courtyard calling out her son's name.

Over the next few days hundreds of civilians and Salt Lake County's search and rescue team joined the hunt for young Daniels. Among the civilians were faculty and students from the University of Utah and members of a local Teamsters union. Descriptions of the child and descriptions of his clothing were printed and broadcast throughout the entire state. Police had questioned hundreds of people to no avail.

That night Bishop drove the corpse in the box to Cedar Fort, 20 miles southwest of Salt Lake City, and buried the child in the desert with only the trees that gave the nearby town its name as his gravestone.

While driving home, Bishop struggled with myriad emotions: revulsion at what he had done, fear of arrest, perverse excitement, and an overriding belief that he would, in fact, kill again unless he sought some type of help.

Kim Peterson, 11

During the year between Daniels' murder and his next one, Bishop pursued what he believed to be a less dangerous outlet for his uncontrollable and deadly urges. He began to kill puppies he adopted from Salt Lake City animal shelters. Such behavior is one aspect of the well-known triad of characteristics common to serial killers with the other two being bedwetting and setting fires. Over a span of 12 months Bishop adopted as many as 20 homeless puppies, essentially using them as surrogates for children. He later told investigators that "it was so stimulating" and that a puppy's whines were just like Daniels' own cries were. He would get frustrated at the puppies and then bludgeon them with hammers, drown them, or strangle them. It is unknown as to whether Bishop's neighbors knew of his activities; however, at the time, animal cruelty was a simple misdemeanor. Once he grew bored and discovered that the puppies failed to satisfy his urges Bishop went back to molesting children; using lures or threats to prevent them from reporting him.

The next young boy to vanish was 11-year-old Kim Peterson. On 8 November 1980, Peterson had spoken to a man about roller skates at the local skating rink with Kim mentioning that he wanted to sell his pair to purchase another. Bishop told the child he would pay him $35 for his skates. The next day, Peterson left home to go to the rink to sell them. Whereas both of Peterson's parents knew that he had found a buyer, neither of them knew who the mystery man was as no names were mentioned.

As Peterson had promised his parents he would come right home after the sale, when he failed to return they called the police and another fruitless search began. Witnesses at the rink reported that a child matching Peterson's description was talking to a white male, approximately 25 to 35 years of age who weighed around 200 pounds and had a full face, dark hair, and glasses, and clad in blue jeans and am army-style jacket was seen talking to Peterson earlier that day. One witness claimed that the man and the boy had driven away in a silver Chevy Camaro with out-of-state license plates; perhaps from Nevada. However, every lead was useless.

At this time, the police saw no similarity between their suspect and the Roger Downs who lived in an apartment a few blocks from the Petersons' home. Whereas they, again, questioned him routinely, they failed to make a connection between Peterson's disappearance and the disappearance of young Daniels the previous year.

Bishop had bludgeoned Peterson to death with a hammer and buried his body in the desert near where he had buried Daniels' body.

At this point, Bishop realized that murder was far easier the second time and surmised that there was plenty of room in the desert to bury children. While he still feared arrest, he spared his victims if they promised not to talk; however, he was discovering the incomparable rush that murder provided him that was better than any drug.

Danny Davis, 4

On 20 October 1981, four-year-old Danny Davis vanished at a busy supermarket in southern Salt Lake County while shopping with his grandmother. Prior to his kidnapping, Bishop (who later told detectives that while browsing through a local grocery store) "saw the most beautiful little boy kneeling in the aisle" as Davis was trying to get a gumball out of one of the store's machines. Bishop offered Davis some candy but the boy refused. As he was leaving the store Bishop happened to glance behind him to see Davis walking in his direction. He waited for the boy and then led him into the parking lot. Davis' grandmother couldn't find him when she had finished shopping and, as would be expected, panicked. Employees and customers searched the store and parking lot but couldn't find the young boy.

Witnesses said that they remembered a small boy near the gumball machine but could not identify photos of Davis. Others recalled a smiling man talking to Davis but could not give a clear description. They also reported that Davis was seen leaving the store with a man and a woman; however, the woman remains unknown. Witnesses also underwent hypnosis; however, while descriptions of the smiling man were clarified no identification could be made.

Police subsequently launched one of the biggest searches in Utah history trying to find the young boy. Fliers were printed with Davis' photo and copies were sent to law enforcement agencies across the country. A $20,000 reward was offered but nobody had any useful leads. Calls to the Federal Bureau of Investigation (FBI), the National Crime Information Center (NCIC), and Child Find were all to no avail.

Despite hundreds of searchers and the FBI scouring nearby neighborhoods, mountains, lakes, and woods, the young boy was never found. Concern increased as Davis was clad only in blue jeans, a t-shit, and thong sandals when last seen and the temperatures were dropping into the 30's at night. After no luck for two days, divers then searched Big Cottonwood Creek, ponds, roadside ditches, and even went through garbage dumpsters in hundreds of alleys.

At the time, Bishop—still under his alias of Downs—lived a mere half a block from the store and, again, was routinely questioned; however, the police still made no connection that the "same clueless neighbor" had lived in close proximity to all of the missing children. In fact, by the time police visited Bishop in his rented house, Davis was already dead.

Bishop molested the young boy and then silenced his crying by manually pinching his nose and covering his mouth until the child died. The following day Bishop, again, drove to Cedar Fort and buried his third victim beside the other two. Bishop believed that he had a foolproof plan as the Salt Lake City Police Department still had no clue.

After the fact—and much too late—neighbors did mention to police that Mr. Downs had an unusual fondness for children.

Bishop had no need for the reward offer as he still had ample money from his latest embezzlement scheme.

While Bishop was, indeed, cunning and was able to keep the police at bay, state legislators sprang into action as a result of numerous child disappearances. In August 1982, three-year-old Rachel Runyan was kidnapped from a school playground in Sunset; a mere 30 miles north of Salt Lake City. Discovery of her strangled corpse led to numerous calls for action by many organizations and the legislature passed another law.

Whereas first-degree murder was already a capital offense in Utah, the growing indignation with child abductions provided the impetus for the state legislature to add mandatory five-, ten-, or 15-year sentences for convicted child abductors. While this action was all fine and dandy it didn't get investigators any closer to finding out who was responsible for the recent missing children.

Eventually investigators dismissed any possible link between Runyan's murder and the missing Salt Lake City boys. However, there was still much speculation with respect to the disappearances of Daniels, Peterson, and Davis. Detectives from both the Salt Lake and Davis County Sheriff's Departments met with city police departments and FBI agents to try to come up with a lead. Since each of the boys had disappeared at different times of the day and on different days, speculation as to the abductor's employment was frustrated. Investigators also dismissed a clear link between the three boys as most killers tend to prey on members of their own race so while Peterson and Davis were Caucasian, Daniels was African-American. Additionally, Peterson was three times older than both Daniels and Davis. Thus any potential for a pedophile who stalked preschool children was dismissed as well.

By June 1983 almost two years had passed since the last child disappeared. That was to change.

Troy Ward, 6

Bishop's fourth victim was Troy Ward who was abducted on 23 June 1983, his sixth birthday. He was taken from a park near his home where he was permitted to play. Ward was supposed to meet a family friend at 4:00 p.m. at a predetermined street corner and the friend would drive him home to a surprise party. However, when 4:00 came and went with no signs of the child the friend drove to the Ward's residence hoping that the child was, perhaps, already there.

Police were immediately called and officers commenced searching the area around the park. One witness remembered seeing a boy who matched Ward's description leaving the scene with a man on foot just prior to 4:00 p.m. The witness assumed them to be father and son as they looked completely at ease with each other.

Of course, that man was Bishop who had just taken his fourth victim back to his home where—not unlike his other victims—Ward was sexually assaulted, bludgeoned with a hammer, and then drowned in the bathtub. Bishop later stated that he initially thought of letting the boy go; however, Ward's last-minute threats to expose Bishop led to his demise.

Afterward, instead of driving to his own private graveyard near Cedar Fort, Bishop drove east and buried the boy near Big Cottonwood Creek in the Twin Peaks Wilderness Area.

Bishop again realized how easy everything was and he decided not to wait another two years to kill again. He waited less than a month.

Graeme Cunningham, 13

On 14 July, 13-year-old Graeme Cunningham disappeared from his home two days before he was planning on attending a camping trip with a junior high classmate and their chaperone: 32-year-old Roger Downs. The boy was excited for his trip and was already all packed. That Thursday afternoon, two days before he was to leave, Cunningham vanished from his neighborhood without a trace; thus prompting his parents to call the police when he didn't come home for dinner.

The abduction made the news and Bishop visited Cunningham's mother to offer any help he could in finding her son. Police drew similarities to John Wayne Gacy who was convicted of murdering and burying under his house 33 victims and was seen talking with the last of his victims before that victim disappeared. The literature is rife with examples of serial killers who let down their guards and committed clumsy and costly mistakes. They wondered if Mr. Downs had committed a similar mistake by offering his help to his fifth victim's mother.

Investigation and Arrest

Bishop was again questioned. However, this time the police began to dig into his background and discovered his close proximity to all of the young male victims as well as an "almost unnatural fondness for neighborhood children." Sergeant Bruce White and Detective Steven Smith offered an invitation for Bishop to come to the police station to help find Cunningham. Veteran homicide detective Don Bell was waiting on their arrival and slowly and surely Bell began to pick apart Bishop's story.

They also discovered he was wanted under another alias, Lynn Jones, for embezzling $10,000 from an employer by writing bad checks in his boss' name before stealing his own personnel file from the office and vanishing. Police utilized the pending embezzlement charge to arrest Bishop to give them more time to investigate his possible link in the young boys' disappearances.

By sundown that day investigators had gotten Bishop to confess to five murders spanning four years.

The following morning Bishop took authorities to the Cedar Fort area where he pointed out the graves where Daniels', Peterson's, and Davis' remains were recovered. Bishop then led police another 65 miles south to Big Cottonwood Creek where Ward's and Cunningham's more recently deceased bodies were unearthed.

Autopsy results showed signs of sexual abuse on Ward's and Cunningham's remains. The other two had been buried far too long to provide any useful similar forensic evidence.

When Bishop's house was searched police discovered a .38 caliber gun, a bloodstained mallet and hammer, dozens of photographs of one of his victims taken after his abduction, and other pictures of nude boys which were framed to avoid their faces and, therefore, conceal their identities. Investigators also recovered a book entitled *100 Ways to Disappear and Live Free* that suggested that Bishop had studied how to be a fugitive from justice.

Additional investigation revealed that Bishop had molested dozens of other young boys over the years but did not kill them. After public announcement that Bishop was in custody and had confessed, the police were inundated with calls from parents who claimed that Bishop molested their children, or the children of acquaintances. His reasons for sparing their lives were never fully uncovered. Whereas a number of parents allegedly knew about Bishop's "activities" none of them had approached police during the four-year search for a child murderer, likely due to the fact that Bishop was a devout Mormon who tried to help disadvantaged children, or, perhaps, these parents did not want to admit or accept what happened to their children.

Bishop was charged with five counts of capital murder, five counts of kidnapping, two counts of forcible sexual assault, and one count of sexually abusing a minor; the sexual abuse evidence only applicable to his two most recent victims. Of course, murder was the charge that truly mattered in that if the state successfully proved its case Bishop would be sentenced to death.

Trial

Bishop's trial commenced on 27 February 1984 and lasted until 19 March.

Deputy County Attorney Robert Stott described Bishop as a "ruthless killer and sexual deviant possessed of 'a scheming, calculating, cunning mind.'" However, Bishop made his crimes sound awfully simple. He had said that one can offer children anything and they would go with complete strangers.

Bishop's defense team was led by Jo Carol Nesset-Sale who had very little realistic hope of getting their client acquitted as his confession alone had guaranteed that he would spend, at least, the rest of his life in prison. Therefore, his attorneys tried to mitigate Bishop's crimes in the hope of replacing first-degree murder charges with manslaughter. They argued that Bishop's emotional and psychological "deficits" drove him to kill and that "for some reason [he was] stuck or fixated with a sexual attraction to little boys. He never outgrew these erotic feelings. He was a lonely, frightened child." These words were later quoted by author Clifford L. Linedecker in his 1990 book *Serial Thrill Killers*.

His attorneys claimed that one of the primary culprits behind Bishop's fixation and deviance was pornography. Dr. Victor Cline was called as an expert witness and testified pornography had warped Bishop's mind to the extent that he was rendered unable to resist his attraction to children or to the murderous urges that followed. Bishop later stated in an interview with the *Salt Lake Tribune* that Dr. Cline's testimony made him realize what he was. He said:

"During my trial ... Dr. Victor Cline testified about the adverse effects of pornography. As I listened to his explanations, I could discern how my own life desires escalated. These normal feelings become desensitized, and they tend to act out what they have seen. So it was with me. I am a homosexual pedophile convicted of murder, and pornography was a

determining factor in my downfall. Somehow I became sexually attracted to young boys, and I would fantasize about them naked...I would need pictures that were more explicit and shortly the images became commonplace and acceptable. Finding and procuring sexually arousing materials became an obsession. For me, seeing pornography was like lighting a fuse on a stick of dynamite. I became stimulated and had to gratify my urges and explode...If pornographic material would have been unavailable to me in my early stages, it is most probable that my sexual activities would not have escalated to the degree they did."

During his trial, the jurors listened to Bishop's taped confession that included admissions that he had molested his victims after their deaths. During the confession he giggled at times, mimicked the final words of some of his victims in a high falsetto voice, and also said that he was glad he was caught because he would have done it again.

Bishop also confessed that his offering help to Mrs. Cunningham was, in fact genuine. He wanted to allay her despair but did not know how to tell her that he had killed her son.

Ultimately, Bishop was convicted of five counts of murder, five counts of kidnapping, and one count of sexual abuse of a minor. Jude Jay Banks condemned Bishop from the bench and told him that state law gave Bishop the choice of execution by firing squad or lethal injection. Without hesitation he chose the latter.

Bishop later wrote a letter to explain his motives, reiterating much of what he said in his interview. He wrote:

"I am a homosexual pedophile convicted of murder, and pornography was a determining factor in my downfall. Somehow I became sexually attracted to young boys and I would fantasize about them naked. Certain bookstores offered sex education, photographic, or art books which occasionally contained pictures of nude boys. I purchased such books and used them to enhance my masturbatory fantasies...Finding and procuring sexually arousing materials became an obsession. For me, seeing pornography was lighting a fuse on a stick of dynamite. I became

stimulated and had to gratify my urges or explode. All boys became mere sexual objects. My conscience was desensitized and my sexual appetite entirely controlled my actions."

Soon after Bishop was sentenced, while on death row at the Utah State Prison at Point of the Mountain, there was a rumor that some unknown people had offered a $5,000 bounty for his murder, as well as another $5,000 for his brother Douglas' head. Prison Security Chief Captain Craig Rasmussen told reporters that these types of rumors occur pretty regularly but they had to take the threats against Bishop seriously because if he were to be attacked or otherwise injured after they had been given the warning then catastrophic results could ensue. There were no attempts on the lives of either of the Bishop brothers; however, their status as "short eyes" (child molesters) rendered them both outcasts within the prison hierarchy.

During this time Bishop was trying to rectify his Mormon beliefs with his current status. He said, "With great sadness and remorse, I realize that I allowed myself to be misled by Satan." This rediscovery of his religion led to a sort of repentance and some hope that he might actually survive, albeit in prison. His attorneys pursued a petition for a new trial but on 3 February 1988 the Utah Supreme Court rejected these efforts. At this time Bishop did, in fact, give up hope and resign himself to death.

On 29 February, Bishop filed a motion to dismiss his attorneys and to replace them with counsel who would be willing to abandon any further appeals. Following another competency hearing, the trial court determined that Bishop knew what he was doing and on 2 May the Utah Supreme Court lifted his indefinite stay of execution and ordered the trial court to set an execution date.

Three days later, Bishop appeared in front of Judge Frank Noel—handcuffed and shackled—and read a brief handwritten statement that said:

"In reflecting back on my life, I remember a lot of good things, but these are overshadowed by the things I have done. I wish I could make restitution somehow, but I don't see how I can. I wish I could go back and change what happened, or that by giving my life these five innocent lives could be restored. Again, I say that I am truly sorry for all the anguish."

Judge Noel was unmoved by Bishop's words and signed his official death warrant, scheduling Bishop's execution for 10 June 1988.

Just prior to his execution, prison psychologist Al Carlisle told reporters that Bishop appeared to be a new man who had read the *Book of Mormon* ten times from cover-to-cover during his four years in prison and wore television headphones to drown out the profanity spewed at him by other inmates. Carlisle also stated that Bishop feared that his old impulses would return if he were ever freed. He added that Bishop demonstrated remorse during his entire time in prison and that Bishop believed that he would be entering the spirit world which will be more peaceful than on Earth. He also stated that Bishop didn't believe that he had been forgiven but he did believe that he could continue to work on his problems "on the other side."

Bishop then told prison officials and guards that he was "ready and anxious to die."

Bishop met with his parents for the final time on 8 June 1988 and then spent the remainder of his time alive by fasting and praying. Mormon Bishop Heber Geurts told *Salt Lake Tribune* reporter Robert Mims that it was unbelievable how calm and cool Bishop was during his final moments alive. Geurts added, "Even the guards can't understand it. I've dealt with thousands of inmates in 33 years, and he's the most sorrowful and repentant and remorseful man I've ever seen."

Whereas Bishop appeared to absolve his soul through his realignment with the Mormon Church and did, in fact, appear on all accounts to be extremely repentant, this neither eliminates nor minimizes the fact that he purposefully abducted five young boys, sexually assaulted them, and then murdered them; in addition to countless other children who he had sexually molested. These five boys are gone forever and their families are left to suffer their losses and Bishop's other victims had their innocence stolen from them; something they will never be able to recover. At least his own recognition of his deviant pedophiliac proclivities and push to stop any and all appeals in order to reach the death chamber as soon as possible did, in fact, serve to save an unknown number of other potential victims.

By 8:00 p.m. Wednesday, 8 June, Bishop had been transferred from his maximum security death row cell to a holding cell a mere 100 feet from the death chamber and, as is commonplace, was placed under 24-hour observation.

Twenty-seven hours later—just before midnight on Friday 10 June, Bishop was escorted into the 24-foot-by-24-foot execution chamber "with practiced precision." He was shackled yet did not resist, fully cooperating with the corrections officers. He was directed to climb onto the gurney that was bolted to the concrete floor in the northwest corner of the room and to stretch out his arms. Bishop did so without any hesitation. Utah Department of Corrections Deputy Director Bruce Egan stated that while Bishop was relaxed about the prospect of dying he was, in fact, "very nervous" about the execution itself.

Bishop forewent the "traditional" last statement to, first, dispel any rumors that he had been sexually molested as a child or had committed other murders and, second, to pray for his fellow man. Bishop said:

"By accepting my execution I do not consider myself a courageous hero or a noble martyr, or that I am giving up or that I'm going out in a blaze of glory, as some people have suggested. I am merely accepting my just punishment as my conscience dictates I must. Though perhaps too little too late, I am doing the right thing now."

As well as:

"I leave this life with no ill feelings towards anyone, and I pray that the peace of God may rest upon each and every one of you. I know of God's

love, patience and compassion, and have found comfort in that knowledge. When I kneel before Christ in the next life, having a perfect recollection of all my guilt, with a broken heart, I will humbly plead, 'Jesus, thou Son of God, have mercy on my soul.'"

Arthur Gary Bishop was ultimately executed smoothly and without flaw on Friday, 10 June 1988. At the time of his execution he expressed remorse for his actions.

By 12:15 a.m.—a mere nine minutes after his execution began—Bishop was pronounced dead by Dr. J. Brett Lazar, director of the Division of Community Health Services. Bishop's body was then taken to the state medical examiner's office for an autopsy before it was released to his family for the cremation Bishop requested.

Aftermath

Interestingly, the fact that Utah offers its condemned prisoners the choice of death by firing squad or lethal injection dates back to the early days of the Mormon Church in the 1850s when Brigham Young and Heber Kimball preached a doctrine of strict "blood atonement." This meant that sinners could demonstrate their repentance by spilling their own blood and if they failed to do so then other church members may be required to assist them. Thankfully, that grim doctrine is largely ignored today except by extremists such as Ervil LeBaron—dubbed the "Mormon Manson"—whose mass-murdering polygamist cult continues to practice it. Double killer Gary Gilmore chose the firing squad for his own execution in 1977 and continues to be the last to choose said method; however, the option remains on the books.

THE BRILLIANT SERIAL KILLER : THE TRUE STORY OF ISRAEL KEYES

MARK TOLBERT

Israel Keyes was an American serial killer who was active from approximately 2001 to his capture in 2012. He was known for his extreme attention to detail, his patience and discipline in selecting targets that lived far away from him. He was also meticulous in disposing of his victim's bodies as authorities have not uncovered any other evidence that Keyes did not provide.

Keyes killed several victims across the United States and was finally caught in 2012 after he uncharacteristically deviated from his modus operandi and hatched a plan to collect a ransom from his last victim's family.

Keyes was known to go to extreme lengths to hide his involvement in these murders, including driving across the country in rental cars, while using nothing but cash and removing the batteries from his cell phones in order to evade detection. This is uncharacteristic for a serial killer, since the vast majority of his contemporaries are known to have killed within their general geographic area.

While in federal custody in Anchorage, Alaska, Keyes would cooperate with investigators and admit to a host of crimes, including kidnapping, rape, and murder. Furthermore, Keyes admitted to committing a variety of burglaries and bank robberies to fund his killing sprees.

Early Life

Israel Keyes was born in Richmond, Utah in 1978. He was the second child to John Jeffrey Keyes and Heidi Hokansson. John, a maintenance man, and Heidi, a stay-at-home mom, raised their son in a Mormon environment and home-schooled both Israel and his eight siblings.

Soon after his birth, Israel's parents moved the family to Aladdin Road, a small area north of Colville, Washington. While his family officially followed the Mormon faith, they were known to attend a local Christian Identity church, an organization rumored follow a white supremacist version of Christianity. Some, however, dispute this label and liken the religion to having parallels with the Amish church.

The family also quickly became friends with the neighbors, the Kehoe family. Chevie Kehoe, the eldest of eight sons, would later become an infamous white supremacist and convicted murderer, after killing William Frederick Mueller, along with his wife and daughter, during a robbery to secure guns, ammunition, and money.

During his time in Aladdin Road, Israel became a very introverted child with little interaction with the other children in town. He built his own cabin at the age of sixteen and preferred the wilderness over people. He is known to have burglarized several houses during his time in Aladdin, however, and is believed to have killed family pets for entertainment.

"When I was fourteen there was some friends staying with us," Keyes recalled. "And there was this cat of ours that was always getting into the trash. I had a lot of guns and I would always carry a gun and I shot it in the stomach. And it ran around and around the tree...and then it like crashed into the tree. I actually kind of laughed a little I think but..and then I looked over at everybody else and the kid who was with me, he was throwing up. Like he was, really, I don't know (chuckles) traumatized I guess you would say."

"Like most serial killers," forensic psychiatrist Paula Orange said. "Keyes built himself up to killing people by killing small animals first."

Following his family's relocation to Smyrna, Maine to become involved in the maple syrup business in the late 1990s, Keyes was kicked out of his family home for rejecting his parents' faith. His parents told his siblings to stay away from him.

"Keyes didn't think too much of his family," Orange said. "He was raised in a cult-like atmosphere and rejected the family religion, becoming very outspoken out his lack of belief in God. He had a Satanic pentagram branded on his back as well as an upside-down cross on his chest."

The rejection made Keyes want to tour the country and burn down as many churches as he could. Instead, he turned to murder and rape.

His first violent crime was committed sometime between 1996 and 1998, when Keyes abducted a teenage girl and raped her. Despite his later penchant for murder, he allowed this victim to go free. The identity of the teenage girl remains unknown.

Military Career

In 1998, Israel Keyes decided to enlist in the United States Army while living in New Jersey. Keyes served as a specialist in the 1st Battalion, 5th Infantry. He was subsequently stationed at Ft. Lewis, near Tacoma, Washington, and at Ft. Hood, near Killeen, Texas. He would later receive training in the Sinai region of Egypt.

While serving in the U.S. Army, Keyes was awarded the Army Achievement Medal for "meritorious service while assigned as a gunner and assistant gunner from the 2nd of December 1998 to the 8th of July, 2001 in the Alpha Company 60mm mortar section." Although Keyes received a DUI in Washington state in May 2001, he left the U.S. Army with an honorable discharge later that year.

Keyes would settle in Alaska and get a job working in construction. Incredibly, he would draw rave reviews from his employer who had no idea of the double life his new carpenter with the long hair led.

"Keyes was described as someone who was very professional," Orange said. "He had a tremendous focus and would work on projects for hours on end with intensity and focus. He would not stop for lunch. He would just work straight on through."

Keyes was described in a favorable manner by just about everyone else who met him. Words like "friendly", "low-key", "reliable" were among the adjectives used to describe him.

"The secret life was power to Israel Keyes," Orange said. "He got off on the fact that everyone he encountered had no idea who or what he really was. To them, he was a friendly carpenter who was on the quiet side. Mellow. But inside he was a raging killer. That is what gave him power."

Crimes

Bill & Lorraine Currier

After receiving his honorable discharge from the United States Army, and sometime between April and May 2011, Israel Keyes constructed a homemade silencer for his Ruger .22 pistol. Once he decided to kill, Keyes booked a flight from Washington state to Indiana. After arriving in Indiana, Keyes rented a car and drove the remaining 1,000 miles to the East Coast of the United States, using cash-only for the duration of the trip to avoid leaving behind any evidence.

Keyes arrived in New York to test his homemade silencer, then traveled to Vermont to pick up a murder "toolkit" that he had buried two years before. Keyes soon found an abandoned farmhouse in Essex, Vermont, which he identified as the location he would take his next victim to before killing them. He initially targeted random drivers passing through the rural area, intending to shoot out a tire on their car and kidnap them after they crashed, but decided to focus on a married couple after dismissing his original plan as unpractical and dangerous.

He soon identified Bill and Lorraine Currier, living at 8 Colbert Street, as his next victims on July 8, 2011.

Bill and Lorraine were 49 and 55 years old respectively. They had just celebrated their 25th wedding anniversary. Bill worked at the local university as a lab assistant while Lorraine worked at a nearby medical center.

"They were good people," Orange said. "They had a lot of pride in the upkeep of their Vermont home, manicuring the lawn and planting flowers. They were good employees and well-liked by co-workers. They were the epitome of upstanding, normal good people."

Keyes had picked the Currier's because they had no dog, no kids and a garage that would let him into the house. He stalked them for days, knowing their comings and going.

As one investigator would note, "Keyes was a serial killer with a system."

In the middle of the night, Keyes disabled the Currier's phone line and entered their house in what has been described as a "blitz attack." He ambushed the couple while they were sleeping and quickly subdued them, tying the couple up and stealing Lorraine's .38 snub-nose revolver in the process.

Once the couple was secured, he proceeded to transport them to the abandoned farmhouse in Essex. During the course of the night, both Lorraine and Bill attempted to escape the house. Lorraine was successfully captured and re-restrained. However, Keyes shot Bill with his silenced .22 caliber Ruger pistol in a fit of rage during his escape attempt. After killing Bill, Keyes sexually assaulted Lorraine and strangled her to death in the basement.

Following the killings, Keyes buried Bill and Lorraine's bodies in the basement of the Essex farmhouse, intending to return to the house at a later date to set fire to the building and thereby destroy any evidence in the blaze. Once the bodies were buried, Keyes set out to commit a robbery spree using the Currier's car.

"Keyes was spotted driving the Currier's car," Orange said. "The eyewitness quickly relayed this information to the police and they were able to come up with a sketch of Keyes. They were reported missing by this time and the authorities knew that foul play was involved. Things became particularly worrisome as the man in Currier's car was driving alone and the couple was nowhere to be found."

The Currier's car soon suffered "serious mechanical issues" and Keyes decided not to go through with his crime spree.

Keyes quickly abandoned the Currier's non working car in an apartment parking lot at 203 Pearl Street and proceeded to the White National Monument Forest to burn the couple's belongings and to bury his toolkit and handgun.

Unbeknownst to Keyes, the farmhouse containing the Currier's bodies was bulldozed from October 25-27, 2011. The bodies, along with the rest of the farmhouse, were unknowingly disposed of at the local landfill.

The resting place lived up to Keyes' motto, 'Out of sight, out of mind.'

Samantha Koenig

On February 1, 2012, Keyes began to search for another random victim. He identified 18-year old barista Samantha Koenig, living and working in Anchorage, Alaska, as his next victim.

Samantha worked at a walk-up kiosk on a relatively busy highway. It was snowing that night, however, and folks were driving by too fast to pay attention to the man who walked up to the counter in a ski mask. This would not be unusual in Anchorage as the weather was freezing. Samantha greeted Israel with a smile and he handed her his travel mug, asking for some coffee. She would turn back around he had a gun pointed at her.

"Turn out the lights," he commanded.

Samantha complied.

"Turn around," he said.

Samantha began to cry, complying with his command. He forced her to empty the register then tied up her wrists with cable wire. After finding out that Koenig had a boyfriend who was set to show up soon, Keyes laid in wait for the boyfriend, Duane Tortolani. However, he quickly abandoned his plan to capture a second victim and dragged Koenig to his truck before transporting her to his property.

The next day, February 2nd, Keyes broke into Koenig's house. While there, he also burglarized her boyfriend's truck, taking the couple's joint debit card with him. However, both Koenig's father and Duane Tortolani witnessed this burglary and notified the authorities.

Keyes quickly tested the debit card to make sure that it worked and, upon confirming that it worked, he returned to his home and quickly killed Koenig, leaving her body in a storage shed located on his property. He immediately traveled to New Orleans, where he set out on a week-long cruise. However, once he disembarked from the cruise Keyes became increasingly concerned over the media coverage and intense police investigation of Keonig's disappearance and set out on a crime spree.

On February 16, Keyes burglarized and burned down a home in Aledo, Texas. Shortly thereafter, Keyes robbed the National Bank of Texas, attempting to kidnap yet another woman he saw walking a dog. Luckily, this potential victim was able to escape.

Other Victims

Israel Keyes is suspected of killing or attempting to kill several other victims. Keyes' first admitted violent crime took place sometime between 1996 and 1998, when he abducted and raped a teenage girl in Washington state. Unlike his later crimes, Keyes did not kill this victim. He released her soon after the sexual assault.

"My entire goal was to stay under the radar," Keyes said. "For a lot of this stuff, there wasn't anything. All I can say is that unless I talk about it, you're never going to find any evidence."

His first suspected murder is of an unknown couple in Washington State in 2001. Keyes also claimed to have killed another unidentified victim in Leah Bay, Washington in July 2001.

He planned out his killings like most people plan out their vacations. He would travel far away from his location.

From 2005 to 2006, Keyes is suspected of killing two separate victims. He confessed to these murders while being held at the

Anchorage Correctional Complex, saying that these murders were committed on two separate occasions. Furthermore, he claimed to have dumped one of the bodies in Crescent Lake, located in Oregon.

"There is a history of this stuff that goes back a long time," Keyes said. "It's not something I've ever talked to anyone about."

Keyes just didn't rape his female victims. He would rape his male victims as well. It was something he was ashamed of as well as his necrophilia.

Following a multi-year break from killing, Keyes admitted to killing Debra J. Feldman in Hackensack, New Jersey on April 8, 2009. He also claimed to have killed another victim the following day somewhere in New York state.

Keyes would bury his murder weapons across numerous fields across the entire United States. Because of his military training, he knew how to maintain the weapons and return to them after they had been out of use for years. He buried these weapons in canisters filled with cable ties, ropes and drain cleaner.

During these trips, Keyes would admit to frequenting prostitutes.

Lastly, following the murder of Samantha Koenig and during his travels throughout the Southwestern United States, Keyes claims to have killed an unknown victim in Texas. The identity and final location of this victim remain unknown.

In addition to the actual murders that he committed, Keyes admitted to attempting to kill several other individuals over the years. For example, Keyes admitted to attempting to shoot both a couple and male police officer in Anchorage, Alaska sometime between April and May 2011. He also admitted to attempting to kidnap and kill a woman he spotted walking her dog in Texas, just days before his capture by a combination of Texas and federal law enforcement.

Other Crimes

Keyes was known to commit burglaries and bank robberies in order to fund his killing sprees. In addition, he admitted to killing small animals from the time he was a young child. He is said to have killed an unknown number of family dogs and cats throughout his travels.

<u>April 10, 2009</u>

Keyes robbed the Community Bank in Tupper Lake, NY in order to fund his killing spree. After holding up the bank teller with a .40 caliber Smith & Wesson (and with a .22 caliber 10/22 Ruger pistol in reserve), Keyes made off with over $10,000 in cash. Although he was filmed on camera during the robbery, his use of sunglasses, uncharacteristic clothing, and a fake mustache prevented him from being identified.

Following the successful robbery, Keyes buried a box with his robbery supplies in the Woodside Natural Area in Essex, Utah. He returned home four days later with the $10,000 in his possession.

<u>February 16, 2012</u>

While Keyes was traversing across the Southwestern United States following the successful ransom for Samantha Koenig, he committed two additional crimes. First, Keyes committed arson by setting fire to and burning down a 3,500 square foot house in Aledo, Texas. Secondly, Keyes again committed a bank robbery by holding up a teller at the National Bank of Texas in Azle, Texas, making off with an undisclosed amount of cash.

In all, Keyes is suspected of committing some 20 to 30 home invasions and burglaries during his lifetime. Furthermore, he killed an unknown amount of animals from his childhood to capture and is believed to have committed several unidentified bank robberies during his adult years in order to fund his killing trips across the country.

Capture

After murdering Samantha Koenig and leaving Alaska, Keyes concocted a plan to demand a $30,000 ransom for Koenig's return (at the time, police were unaware that Koenig had been killed). Keyes texted his demands and instructions to Duane Tortolani, Koenig's boyfriend.

At the same time, Keyes dug up the body of Samantha Koenig, dismembered it, and disposed of the body in Matanuska Lake.

The case became a high-profile one and community members chipped in to meet the ransom demand.

Thirty-thousand dollars, courtesy of a concerned and frightened community, would be deposited into Samantha's account.

After receiving the ransom money, Keyes began withdrawing cash from the associated account using her stolen debit card. There would be withdrawals in Alaska. Then Arizona. Then New Mexico.

The authorities would always be fifteen minutes behind the suspect when he made these withdrawals.

Israel would wear a "Scream" mask while the withdrawals but his 2012 Ford Focus that he was drawing was identified. The FBI noted all of their counterparts to be on the lookout for Keyes in this vehicle. It is important to note that Keyes actually exchanged his rented 2012 Ford Focus for another car to avoid detection; however, the rental company provided him with another 2012 Ford Focus for his exchange. This would eventually help to lead to his capture.

Police were then able to track account withdrawals as he traveled throughout the Southwestern United States, having made withdrawals from Koenig's account using her debit card in New Mexico, Arizona, and Texas. Interestingly, authorities had a video of Koenig's abduction but refused to release the footage to the public, a controversial move that many outsiders saw as hampering his capture.

Having left his sister's wedding just days before (where he became embroiled in a contentious argument about his pronounced atheism), Keyes was spotted speeding along Highway 59 by a Texas Highway Patrolman on March 13, 2012.

"The patrolman that made the traffic stop had no idea that Keyes was a wanted serial killer," Orange said "Keyes did not have his gun handy at the time. If he had, there's no doubt in my mind that he would have started shooting."

Keyes was placed under arrest by the patrolman and the Texas Rangers as well as the FBI was brought in. Authorities found the following items in Keyes' possession at the time of his capture: Koenig's ATM card and cell phone (with the battery removed), a ski-mask, handgun, and bundles of rubber-banded cash that was traced to the recent National Bank of Texas robbery.

The authorities still had hope that Samantha was still alive.

But Keyes would tell them nothing. He stared straight ahead without emotion as detectives hammered him with questions. Authorities would get very little out of him. He was thirty-four years old and lived a quiet life with his girlfriend and ten year old daughter in Anchorage. Everything about Keyes' past seemed normal. But he had a creepy withdrawn nature about his personality. When the FBI searched his property, they found out why.

He had searched numerous time on his computer for Samantha Koenig. The FBI would then confront Keyes with the surveillance footage they had of his truck pulling up in front of the kiosk.

"We know it was your truck," the FBI agent said.

Keyes would remain silent for about forty seconds before he finally spoke.

"Well, I might as well tell you everything. She's dead."

Keyes revealed that he had used a needle and thread to open up Samantha's eyes as she posed with the newspaper in the ransom photo.

Keyes would recount how he brought Samantha back to his home and tied her up. He had a glass of wine before he began verbally taunting Samantha by telling her what he was going to do to her. He then raped the victim and choked her to death.

Only twenty feet away, his live-in girlfriend and ten year old daughter were sleeping. They would wake up the following morning and he would join them at the breakfast table. Like turning a switch on-and-off, he spoke of taking his family on a cruise.

"It was apparent that neither his girlfriend or his daughter knew of his crimes," Orange said. "He would tell investigators that 'no one really knew him.'"

Shortly after Keyes' capture in Lufkin, he was then extradited to Alaska to stand trial for Koenig's murder. His trial was set for March 2013 and he was slated to be represented by federal defender Rich Curtner. Keyes was thirty-four years old at the time of his arrest.

Investigation

Israel Keyes was officially extradited to Alaska on March 26, 2012. Shortly after arriving at the Anchorage Correctional Complex, Keyes confessed to the murder of Samantha Koenig, providing information which allowed investigators to locate her dismembered body on April 1st of the same year.

Keyes was initially willing to cooperate with authorities and offered to confess and plead guilty to all charges leveled against him if two terms were met: his trial would last no longer than one year and he would be given the death penalty. He also conditioned his cooperation on the basis that his name and certain details not be released to the media and public.

"I'm not in this for the glory," Keyes told interrogators. "I'm not trying to be on TV. I want my kid to have a chance to grow up. She's in a safe place now, she's not going to see any of this. I want her to have a chance to grow up and not have this hanging over her head."

In June 2012, Keyes attempted to violently escape from a courthouse in Anchorage, in what authorities suspected was a spur-of-the-moment suicide attempt. Keyes was successfully subdued with a taser and taken back into custody alive. Following his attempted escape, Keyes was placed on a suicide watch, which entailed a prohibition on razor blades and sharp objects, regular inspections of his cell, and a 24/7 guard.

The next month, in July 2012, a local news station, WCAX, reported Keyes' connection to the kidnapping and murder of the

Curriers. This lead to Keyes ending all cooperation with the authorities for the next two months.

Modus Operandi

While cooperating with authorities at the Anchorage Correctional Complex, Keyes described his approach to killing thusly: "I would let them come to me... You might not get exactly what you're looking for, there's not much to pick from, so to speak. But there's also no witnesses, there's nobody else around."

Location

Israel Keyes was very methodical in his approach to killing. Unlike most serial killers, Keyes did not kill victims who lived near him. Most serial killers conduct most of their kidnapping and abductions within the vicinity of their home, which leads to an easier investigation and higher chance of being captured. Keyes, on the other hand, was known to take cross-country trips in order to kill.

For example, Keyes killed the Curriers in Vermont while he was living in Washington state. Once he decided to kill, Keyes booked a flight from Washington to Indiana. He then rented a car, removed the battery from his cell phone, and paid for all of his expenses with cash as he drove 1,000 miles to the East Coast. He tested his homemade silencer in New York, retrieved a murder toolkit that he had hidden in Vermont two years earlier, and then identified the Curriers as his next victims. This type of careful planning, attention to detail, and restraint is very uncommon in serial killers.

Victim Profile

Unlike most serial killers, Keyes did not have a specific victim profile. For instance, Ted Bundy, another serial killer who shared many qualities with Keyes, was known to target young, white women between the ages of 15 and 25. However, Keyes had no such victim profile. He alternatively killed or attempted to kill married couples, young woman, men, and several other unknown victims. This allowed him to operate without substantial police scrutiny for some time.

Method of Killing

With the exception of his killing of Bill Currier, Keyes strangled every one of his victims. Furthermore, Bill Currier was shot to death while attempting to escape from the house that Keyes was keeping him and his wife at. Had Bill not been killed in the heat of passion while attempting to escape, it is likely that Keyes eventually would have strangled him to death as well.

Death

After accidentally being provided with razors while on suicide watch, Keyes committed suicide on December 2nd, 2012. He sliced his wrists vertically and hung himself while being held at the Anchorage Correctional Complex. He was pronounced dead immediately.

Prior to committing suicide, Keyes composed a four-page, handwritten letter that was found underneath his body. The letter was covered in blood and was largely illegible, but FBI forensic investigators were able to reconstruct much of his letter.

While the letter did not provide additional details about his crimes and victims, it did offer a glimpse into his psyche and reasons for committing murders. Keyes wrote "Family and friends will shed a few tears, pretend it's off to heaven you go. But the reality is you were just bones and meat, and with your brain died also your soul." Later in his letter he elaborated, "You may have been free, you loved living your lie, fate had its own scheme crushed like a bug, you still die." He repeatedly referred to his victims as a "pretty captive butterfly."

Dr. Stephen Montgomery, a forensic psychiatrist at Vanderbilt University Medical Center analyzed the letter and reached the following conclusion: "It has no remorse, no regard for human life or the victims and that fits with that type of psychopathic personality."

Authorities are still investigating various unsolved disappearances throughout the various states that Keyes visited. It is now believed that he may have targeted homeless shelters where he could kill people who would not be missed.

THE MURDER OF MICHELE AVILA

AIMEE BARNES

Michele Yvette Avila, known as Missy to her friends and family, was born in Los Angeles California in 1968. She grew up 20 miles north of L.A. in Arleta with her mother Irene and three brothers; Ernie, Mark, and Chris. She was the focus of two books, a movie starring Patty Duke as her mother, and several TV shows. However, it was not her life that was remarkable but rather her death. At the tender age of 17, just as her life was beginning, she was murdered.

As horrible as any murder is, this one was made more heinous by the fact that Missy was murdered by those she trusted most, her best friends. The same girls whom she had grown up with on their quiet street in Arleta. Girls she had trusted implicitly with her deepest secrets. That is why the story of Missy's murder must start years before it happens when she was just eight years old when the new girl moved with her family into the house right around the corner from her own.

Karen Severson was that new girl and Missy was the first to befriend her.

Shy, awkward Karen moved into the house right around the corner from the Avila house. Missy invited Karen to her home to play dolls and the two became fast friends. They could often be seen walking arm-in-arm to school or jumping rope and sharing secrets under the willow tree in the Avila front yard.

"Then at 11:30 I went to my friends house. We played barbies, then we went swimming. After we had gone swimming, we played barbies again. Then we went swimming for a long time. (My friends name is Karen.)" This quote from Missy's diary on August 31, 1978 is typical of the other entries surrounding it. In fact, throughout the pages shared by Shavaun Avila, Missy's sister-in-law, Karen is mentioned in the same way on all but one page.

While Laura Doyle had been Missy's friend since long before Karen moved in, she was never as close to Missy as Karen had become. Karen often involved herself in anything Missy and Laura were doing. She seemed jealous of the friendship.

In junior high, both girls fell in with a drinking, drugging crowd of kids. Mark Avila, one of Missy's brothers, was quoted by the Los Angeles Times as saying, "She fell in with a bad crowd. She had to have low self-esteem to hang around with people like that."

By the time Missy and Karen reached 10th grade, events had begun to divide them. While Missy blossomed into a green-eyed beauty, Karen gained weight and began her long relationship with the green-eyed monster. It was that very jealousy which led to the sundering of the friendship and eventually to Missy's death.

Karen craved the attention Missy received. More than one person was quoted saying Karen was obsessed with Missy and wanted to be her. However, Missy was the complete opposite of Karen. Missy was outgoing, popular, and pretty. Karen was overweight, shy, and would have been completely unknown to fellow students if not for Missy. This just made Karen angrier. She blamed Missy for her lack of popularity and began trying to sabotage Missy's.

In one incident, Missy was beaten up by a group of girls who believed a rumor that she had slept with their boyfriends. One of the girls told Missy shortly after the attack that it had been Karen who started the rumor. Still fiercely loyal to her friend, Missy refused to believe that Karen would do that. "Missy was so mad at the girl for telling her it was Karen's fault. Missy 'knew' Karen would never do anything like that." Irene Avila would later say. "Missy made great lasagna, dreamed of becoming a physical therapist, and was fiercely loyal to her childhood friends."

In her junior year, Missy dated a boy named Randy. After a month, she broke up with him because he liked to drink and do drugs too much. He soon started dating Karen and they moved into an apartment together. This soon became party central despite the fact that Karen had given birth to a baby girl she named Stephanie after her sister and that infant was present. Missy told her mother of an incident where Randy pulled her onto his lap just as Karen walked in. Missy quickly got up and told Randy she wasn't interested in dating him again. She suggested Karen leave him. "Karen was really upset because the guy she wanted didn't want her," recalls Irene. "He wanted Missy."

In a similar incident, Laura Doyle's boyfriend, Victor Amaya, had broken up with her due to her constant jealousy. "I broke off the relationship because she was jealous of me talking to other girls, including Missy. Laura refused to accept the breakup and became bitter." Victor would later say.

One day, Laura's drives by Victor's while he and Missy are holding hands and kissing at the end of his driveway. Enraged, she pulls down her window to tell them that they were caught and call Missy names like 'slut' and 'whore.' Instead of apologizing and denying any feelings for Missy as Laura had expected him to, Victor tells her to go away. "We (he and Missy) argued with Laura at my house in Arleta. Me, my brother Noah and Missy had been standing in front of the house when Laura drove up. Laura wanted to know 'Why is Missy here?' and I ordered Laura to leave. Before she drove away she said 'I'm going to kill that bitch!' I didn't take the threat seriously and I never reported it to police."

By September 1985, both Karen and Laura had stopped speaking to Missy. She was divested by the loss of her two closest friends. On September 21st, Karen sees Missy at a local park and attacks her with a beer bottle. She slaps and pushes her former confidant before friends break up the fight. Missy's mother heard of the confrontation but did not later connect it to her daughter's murder. After all, the girls had often quarreled during their long friendship.

"Her only problem, at least on that fateful day was that she was very popular with the boys and this drove Laura Doyle and Karen Severson crazy." Deputy District Attorney Tamia Hope said at the trial. "They started out yelling at her, telling her how mad they were at her, and how she slept with entirely too many boys and messed up entirely too many relationships."

Shortly after that confrontation, the girls apologize to Missy and make up. According to her mother, her excitement was easily noticeable. She is thrilled to have her two best friends back in her life.

On October 2nd, Missy told her mother she was going out with Laura. "When Laura got to the house, the girls were laughing and talking about boys. As they drove off they seemed very carefree. I remember how especially pretty Missy looked that day. She was all excited to go. She even turned to me and said "I love you" which is something she did not ordinarily do. That scene haunts me even today."

They met up with Karen and her roommate Eva Chirumbolo at Stonehurst Park in Sun Valley. From there they drove in two separate cars to Wicky up, also known as Colby Canyon. A spot all three girls were familiar with as it was a popular party spot for teens. A campground in the Angeles State Forest a 45 minute drive from Arleta.

"Karen said that she and Laura 'planned to scare Avila.' I didn't know what they had planned. I didn't know how far this was going to go." Eva would later say at Laura and Karen's trail.

What happened next is pieced together by the three girls testimony. When they reach the forest, they park in a dirt lot near a wooded area near the creek. Laura and Karen get out of their vehicles and begin yelling at Missy who is still sitting in Laura's car. Missy begins crying and the girls force her out of the car and begin pushing her around calling her names and accusing her of stealing their boyfriends.

Eva says she decided to get out of the vehicle as by this point the confrontation was becoming increasingly intense. Missy, who had just been laughing and listening to music with who she believed were her best friends was not crying and noticeably shaking with fear. Laura grabs her wrist and forcibly pulls her towards a trail into the wooded area. Missy resists until Karen comes up and pushes her.

"All four of us walked down an embankment to the creek. Laura and Karen continued screaming at Missy," says Eva, the prosecution's star witness. She continues her retelling of that fateful night's events by saying Laura yanks Missy by her hair and accuses her of sleeping with Victor. She steps up to the creek and pushes Missy towards Karen who shoves her to the ground.

Missy is frantic and begs for forgiveness and frantically pleads for her life. At this point, Eva says she became terrified of what was to come and runs back to the car. "I was scared so I ran back to where the cars were parked," says Eva. She hears Missy scream for her to help her but she feels helpless and feared for her own life. Unlike the obese Karen and aggressive Laura, both Missy and Eva are petite and no physical match for either girl let alone both of them at once.

Karen and Laura continue to beat and batter Missy. One of her earrings is ripped from her ear and becomes tangled in her hair. Her beautiful waist length hair is hacked at with some sharp instrument and clumps of it litter the ground. Laura shouts, "You're going to pay for what you've done! You're going to pay for sleeping with our boyfriends!"

They carry the 98 pound Missy, as she struggled to escape, down to the shallow water, a mere 8 inches deep. As she continues to struggle they forcefully hold her head under the water. They continued to hold her head underwater for several minutes after she quit struggling and then carry a 4-foot, 100 pound log over and put it on her neck to keep her head under the water.

Still scared, Eva asked Laura several times, "What happened? Where's Missy?" She was told that she was drowned. She testified that while both Laura and Karen appeared jittery after the murder but they weren't sorry they had done it. "A few minutes later, Karen and Laura joined me. Karen Severson jumped into her car and drove away. When I got into the car with Laura, she said 'We killed Missy.' Then she said, 'Missy deserved to die because she slept with Victor.'"

Four hours after the murder, Laura called the Avila house and asked to speak with Missy. Irene was confused. "I told her I thought Missy was with her," she says. Laura informed her that she'd dropped Missy off to talk with three boys in a blue Camaro while she went to get gas. When she came back, Missy and the boys were gone.

Three days later, on October 5th, hikers found Missy's body right where the girls had left her, face down in the creek with a log anchoring her in the water. One of the first policemen on the scene said, "The young woman's body was a terrifying sight." Her face was badly beaten and her hair was chopped off.

When the police came to inform Irene Avila that they had found Missy, she collapsed. At the funeral, she collapsed again and had to be rushed to the hospital by ambulance. The grisly murder of her only daughter was simply too much for Irene to bear. Both Karen and Laura attended the funeral of their 'best friend.' Eva Chirumbolo did not.

Shortly after the funeral, Karen and her 2-year-old daughter moved in with Irene. Karen vowed to find the 'animal' that murdered her friend and 'helped' Irene track down clues. She lived with Irene for three months sitting up nights sharing memories of Missy. Irene Avila said, "She was close to me, like another daughter. Karen was my daughter's best friend. They grew up together."

Karen was obsessed with the murder. She visited Missy's grave two or three times a week, often leaving balloons or flowers. The walls of her bedroom with pictures of her dead friend and newspaper articles about her murder. Worse, she began frequently visiting the scene of the murder and was seen sitting by the creek drinking beer.

The cover up began falling apart when Karen announced out of the blue that Laura wanted to change her story. Karen then summoned Laura to Irene's house where she told Missy's mother that she had lied. There was never any blue Camaro or any boys. She now claimed that the truth was she had dropped Missy off near a L.A. church to deliver $500 to a drug dealer.

Not long after that Karen claimed that Missy was haunting her. She claimed to see her sitting on the Avila's couch, floating over her while she slept, and even keeping her car from starting while visiting Missy's grave.

The mystery of who murdered Missy Avila might have never been solved if it weren't for the suicide of Eva Chirumbolo's brother which made her understand the loss the Avila family felt. She finally came forward in July of 1988 and told police everything. She was not charged as an accessory to murder in exchange for her full cooperation.

Based on her recounting of the events, Karen Severson and Laura Doyle were arrested and charged with 1st degree murder. Their trial date was set for September 18, 1989. Both women plead 'not guilty' and Karen told officers, "I know the details of what happened to Missy but I'm not going to say."

Irene's grief is worsened by the shock of having intimately shared it with the woman who caused it. "She was Missy's best friend," says Irene, "but she was jealous of Missy's family, Missy's looks, Missy's popularity and even Missy's relationship with me." Missy's brother Mark, 24, agrees. "Karen, wanted to be Missy," he said to People.

Yet if Karen had been full of love and hate, jealousy and guilt, she kept it hidden. "We talked to Karen several times during the investigation," says L.A. Deputy Sheriff Bill Patterson, "and not once—I mean never—did we suspect she was in on the murder."

"When they told me that it was Karen and Laura, I didn't believe the cops," Avila said. "I couldn't believe it. I couldn't believe it."

Irene never suspected Karen either, it was beyond her comprehension that someone so close to Missy could have been involved in the killing. "Who knows, maybe Missy was haunting Karen to make her pay for what she did," says Irene. "If it's possible, then I hope to God she's haunting her each night in prison."

On January 31, 1990 both Laura Doyle and Karen Severson, both now 22, were convicted of 2nd degree murder. The prosecutor pushed hard for a 1st degree murder conviction saying, "Our position was that this crime was a deliberate, well-planned torture and execution of Missy, and needed to be treated as such," one prosecutor told the Daily News 11 years ago, after Doyle's parole was denied. However, several jurors said afterwards that they and not been convinced that the murder was planned in advance rather than a crime of passion.

Both women received 15 years to life. Karen served her time at the California Institution for Women in Corona, California. Laura, however, was sent to Valley State Prison for Women in Chowchilla, California.

They first became eligible for parole in 1997. During parole hearings, Karen admits she arranged the walk in the woods but says she only planned to torment Missy. Laura also becomes more forthright at her parole hearings and in 2002 she admits to coaxing Missy into the water and killing her but insists that Karen was the ringleader.

During her incarceration, Karen is described as the modal inmate. She was active in self-help groups, Bible studies, tutoring fellow inmates, and earned a Bachelor of Arts degree in psychology and a doctorate in theology. She was also diagnosed with Multiple Sclerosis during her time in prison.

On July 8, 2011, the parole board recommended Karen Severson's release despite the Avila family's objections. Irene Avila was not able to attend this parole hearing for health reasons. After a 2001 parole hearing for Karen, Irene suffered a heart attack and was ordered by her doctors to never attend another one.

Karen's parole was subject to a four month board review period and then the governor has a chance to intervene. While prosecutors say their hands are tied, the Avila family held out hope and began collecting letters opposing her release to send to Governor Brown.

None of their attempts were successful however, and Karen was release on parole. Upon hearing of Severson's release, Irene Avila said, "I wish that girl would die. I feel bad for my sons. I feel bad for everybody who knew her. This was a terrible injustice, a terrible injustice. I don't understand why people who commit murder, they let 'em out." Laura Doyle was paroled shortly after Karen Severson.

The wounds of loss were ripped wide open with the release of Missy's murders. "I hate her. I hate her. I hate her," said Irene Avila, now 72 upon hearing of Laura Doyle's release. "Both should have suffered the death penalty. They are free. My daughter is in the ground."

One would think the story ends there, but it does not.

Despite public outcry, Karen Severson wrote a memoir about the case entitled "My Life, I Lived It." In the memoir, she recounts explicit details of the murder. When asked about the memoir, Karen said, "I walked away. They don't have a daughter. They don't have a sister. I don't have a friend."

When told that there were several other ways she could make money, Karen said, "Like what, sell myself?" Severson told those who questioned the morality of her making money off of her crime that she would donate a portion of the proceeds to an anti-bullying group.

When asked why she does not donate all of the proceeds, Severson responded, "I didn't say everything. I have to live. It's hard to get a job out there."

Unfortunately the 1st Amendment says criminals cannot be prevented from telling their stories. However, the Avila family filed a wrongful death civil lawsuit against Severson and the book's distributor for slander and infliction of emotional distress.

"Today we're filing a lawsuit against a vicious killer who has been profiting off her crime," Shavaun Avila, Missy's sister-in-law told news sources outside court. "It's not about us making money off this lawsuit, it's about letting the public know that crime is paying in California."

In addition to the civil lawsuit, the Avila family pushed legislation in the state assembly called "Missy's Law." It's intended to help family members of crime victims recoup money from a perpetrator who has made money from a book or movie deal based on their crime. The bill was sponsored by State Assembly member Nora Campos.

"This law should have been passed a long time ago," Irene Avila said. "It's like they're giving them a reward for killing somebody."

In response to public outcry and the pending lawsuits, the distributor of Karen Severson's book changed the price to zero, ensuring she would never profit from it.

On October 15th, 2015 Governor Jerry Brown of California passed Missy's Law. The family celebrated it as a huge victory. "I feel like we've won a really big battle, but there's still a war going on out there, and we're going to keep battling as long as it takes," said Shavaun Avila.

For her part, Irene Avila has this to say, "All I can say is, `Girls, watch out whom you trust.'"

SPREE KILL : THE TRUE STORY OF GEORGE BANKS

ANA BENSON

Spree killers are a special kind of murderers who are completely different from serial killers. They commit two or more murders in a short period of time. This means that they do not experience the cooling-off period which is typical for a serial killer. As a matter of fact, their killing spree is often quick and pretty violent.

Driven by an uncontrollable rage, spree killers would often turn on their families, co-workers, or any group of people that wrong them in any way. What triggers these crimes? The debate is still ongoing but it is usually connected with a major event in a killer's life such as a breakup or an argument with someone who is more superior to them.

So when George Banks, a former prison guard, began his rampage in Jenkins Township, Pennsylvania, the entire police force went out to hunt him and try to prevent his further unraveling. Unsure what started his killing spree, they weren't ready for the crime scenes he left behind. They knew he had military training since he worked at a prison and that catching him would be a problem. The law enforcement also realized that they are dealing with a highly psychotic individual that simply had nothing to lose.

So what exactly happened on that autumn day in 1982 and why did George Banks turn on those who were closest to him?

Early life

George Banks was born on 22nd of June, 1942 in Wilkes-Barre, Pennsylvania. He was a mixed race due to the fact that his father, John Mack was African American, while his mother Mary Yelland, was Caucasian. His parents were not married and he was born out of wedlock which was not well received back in that time. Since George Banks was multiracial, his childhood was particularly rough and he was often bullied by his peers. The abuse would be focused on his racial background but it did sometimes involve the lack of a father figure in his life.

He was quite smart but George Banks didn't excel in school. Banks attended St. Mary's Catholic School. He was simply unable to express himself properly so he would get bad grades as a result. It was clear that he will not be going to a college after the high school so he chooses a different path. George Banks made a decision to enroll in the Army 1959. Banks was unable to control his temper back then which led to numerous fights and disputes with both fellow soldiers and his superiors. He didn't care about a rank and would often argue with the officers. He was discharged from the army in 1961. Disappointed with his life so far, Banks decided to stop being an upstanding citizen and get involved with crime.

Banks was only nineteen when he and his gang entered Brazil and Roche tavern with an intention to rob the cash register and take everything they could find of value. The owner of the tavern happened to be inside because he was cleaning up the bar and he didn't have any weapon to defend himself with. After noticing the owner, George Banks aimed his gun and shot him. The owner didn't die but he was badly injured. Banks was arrested shortly afterward. The sentence was six to fifteen years in a State Correctional Institution. He spent eight years in Graterford prison but was paroled in 1969.

After the time he spent behind the bars, George Banks wanted to live his life to the fullest so he married his friend Doris Jones as soon as he got released from the prison. He was set on changing his ways and starting a family was the first step. The marriage lasted for seven years and the couple welcomed two daughters. However, George did physically abuse Doris Jones and their fights often got pretty violent. Banks was unfaithful to her and had many lovers during the time they were married. Doris simply couldn't take it anymore but surprisingly she wasn't the one who filed for a divorce. As a matter of fact, Banks did so in 1976. When the paperwork was completed, Banks felt like a free man. He wanted to go out and date other women without the weight of a marriage on his shoulders.

He preferred Caucasian women after his separation from Doris Jones and he did have one long-term relationship with a woman called Sharon Mazillo. But he was still a cheater and would often have more than one lover on the side. He purchased a house in Wilkes-Barre and began making his own little harem. He had four girlfriends living with him at one point. Banks had at least one child with each and every lover. It seemed that this kind of lifestyle didn't bother the women so they continued to live with Banks for years.

Banks' house was located in a white neighborhood and he claimed that the relations between him and the people who lived on the same street were very intense. The fact that he was African-American was apparently a huge problem. His neighbors didn't agree with his group of lovers either. Banks' children were also the targets of racial hatred according to him. He would later comment on that by saying: "They attempted to burn my house, smashed several windows, squirted my babies with water when they were in the yard and intimidated the girls and children."

On the other hand, his former neighbors told the authorities that Banks and his family mostly kept to themselves. They refused to communicate with the families who lived nearby and Banks would always scold both his girlfriends and children for talking to them. Banks didn't want them to socialize and he controlled their movement.

In 1980, Banks got employed by State Correctional Institute Camp Hill. It was also located in Pennsylvania. He got accepted to the position of a watchtower guard. Somehow his criminal records were overlooked and George Banks became a figure of authority, working on the side of the law this time. But after a couple of months, the changes in his behavior were more than obvious. He was a bit obsessed with famous cult leaders such as Charles Manson and Jim Jones. Banks would also start reading various survivalist publications back then and it looked like he was preparing for some type of racial war.

He started his mental downfall in 1982 and talked excessively about the previously mentioned racial war. He shared his thoughts with the fellow prison guards who would later testify that Banks told them that the conflict will not be avoided and that he wanted to spare his mixed race children from the possible hate they would experience in the process. He wanted to shield them from the hatred he felt when he was younger.

George Banks received a suspension from his work in September of 1982 because he got into a fight with his boss. His treats also involved suicide and he locked himself in a guard tower saying that he would take his own life. The colleagues intervened and they managed to calm Banks down. The whole situation was unusual because it appeared that Banks experienced a full mental breakdown. He was put on a leave of absence until he recovers.

Banks was asked to visit a psychiatrist in a local hospital who might help him with his problems. He ignored the recommendation and the possible help he could have gotten from the doctors. Banks continued his downward spiral into psychosis and started obsessively thinking about killing his girlfriends and children. His paranoid thoughts about the racial war consumed him on a daily basis. Unfortunately, the tragedy was just a couple of weeks away and even though there were plenty of warning signs, nobody prevented it.

Schoolhouse Lane murders

The evening of 24th September 1982 didn't seem even a bit out of the ordinary in Banks household which was located on 28 Schoolhouse Lane. George consumed large quantities of alcohol and prescription pills. He felt powerless over the fact that he was suspended from his job a couple of weeks ago. Plus, his ex-girlfriend Sharon Mazzillo didn't want to give him the full custody of their son, Kissamayu Banks. George was the primary caregiver but Sharon didn't let him take the child into his home so he was living with the mother at a trailer park. After a couple of hours, he closed the door to his bedroom and went to sleep.

Banks woke up early the next morning, took his AR-15 semi-automatic rifle which was by his bed and entered the living room. Regina Clemens, Susan Yuhas, and Dorothy Lyons who were Banks' girlfriends were sitting on the couch, talking with each other. He raised and pointed his rifle, shooting Regina first. The bullet went through her head. Remaining two women were clearly in shock and disbelief because neither of them even tried to run and hide from Banks. Instead, they continued to sit down, staring at Banks.

George Banks then shot Susan five times. The bullets hit her stomach and abdomen. Dorothy was next and she had three bullet wounds on her arms, neck, and torso. The wounds indicated that she tried shielding her face from the attack. Banks moved on to find his children, who were in a nearby room. He shot his twenty months old daughter Mauritania once in the head. Boende who was four years old was killed in the same way.

The rest of Banks' children were upstairs sleeping so he climbed the stairs and found six years old Montanzima in her bed. She received a gunshot to her chest and didn't even wake up when Banks entered the room. Nancy Lyons who wasn't Banks' daughter slept in the bed beside

Montanzima. She was shot twice in her arm and chest. Foraroude was Banks' final victim on Schoolhouse Lane and he was just one year old. Banks placed his rifle on the back of the boy's neck and delivered the fatal shot.

Even though George Banks murdered his entire family that was present at the house, he still had some unfinished business. He went into his bedroom and changed his bloody clothes. Banks selected military fatigues and a T-shirt that had a chilling sentence on the front – Kill em all and let God sort them out. His killing spree did not end there because he had another location to visit.

He exited the house in a hurry and bumped into Jimmy Olsen and Raymond Hall Jr. They were just leaving their home which was on the other side of the street but Banks though of them as possible witnesses who would call the authorities and have him turned in. He had the rifle in his hand and since both of them already saw him, made a decision to shoot the men. Both Olsen and Hall were hit in the chest. Hall died on the spot but Olson did manage to get to the hospital in time and survive the attack because his gunshot wounds weren't life threatening.

Heather Highlands Mobile Home Park murders

Sharon Mazzillo moved into Heather Highlands Mobile Home Park after her breakup with George Banks. She lived there with their son Kissamayu and her mother would often come by in order to help with the child. George Banks drove straight to the mobile home park and burst through the door. He shot Sharon in the chest as soon as she saw her, leaving no time for an argument. Sharon's mother run to the phone as George made his way to his son's room.

Kissamayu was sleeping and he placed the barrel on his son's forehead. The fatal shot was delivered only a couple of seconds later. He returned to the living quarters where Sharon's mother was attempting to call for help and fired the rifle into her head. He then noticed

Sharon's nephew Scott who was staying with them that morning. Scott was crying and was upset after witnessing the murders. George didn't hesitate for a moment, hit the boy with his rifle and continued to scream saying that the boy was bullying Kissamayu because he was half African-American. He then shot him in his head, right behind the boy's ear.

George Banks exited the trailer but he didn't notice Sharon's brother who was hiding in the closet during the entire incident. He found the phone and called the authorities who arrived soon after. Since he was familiar with the lawsuit and knew who George Banks was, Sharon's brother told the police everything he knew about the crime, including the name of the killer.

The police have already found Olsen and Hall back on Schoolhouse Lane and connected Banks to those shootings as well because they knew he was one of the neighbors living on that street. There was no need to hesitate anymore so they entered Banks' home. The police officers who were on the scene were shocked to discover a total of nine bodies inside the house. The house looked like something out of a horror movie and the only living thing inside was the family's dog who was constantly barking. Now they were sure that the killer was extremely dangerous and that they need to find him as soon as possible.

Banks drove away and made a decision to ditch his own car. He stole another vehicle and searched for a place to rest. He finally settled for a secluded parking lot, exited the car and lay down in tall grass. George Banks slept for a couple of hours undisturbed and went straight to his mother's house after he woke up. He told her what he had done and she was in disbelief. Banks' mother called his house in order to check if he was telling the truth or not. The police answered the phone and Banks started talking to them after a couple of minutes.

The police wanted to know more about the crime but they also needed to locate him because they feared he might continue his killing spree. Banks realized what they were doing so he quickly hang up the phone. He gathered up his things, found more bullets for his rifle and drove off to an abandoned house in a less populated area. His friend used to live there so he knew that no one was currently residing there. In the meantime, the law enforcement reached his mother's house and talked to the woman herself. She told them everything she knew, including Banks' current location.

Banks was completely surrounded in the abandoned house by over one hundred officers and the police tried to make him surrender. His mother was driven there by the law enforcement as well, negotiating with Banks. Since they knew he was well armed, they attempted to make him come out by saying that his children did survive the shootings and that they needed his own blood for transfusion. Nothing worked and the police stood outside for hours, wrecking their brains about possible strategies that would make Banks surrender.

They contacted Robert Brunson who was Banks' best friend and a fellow prison guard. He talked to him and finally made Banks exit the house with his hands in the air. The standoff was over without any additional shootings. Banks was taken straight to the police station and received various charges which included eight first degree murders, theft, robbery, assault, and attempted murder.

Chief Detective Jim Zardecki who was at the scene that day would later say: "I looked at him, handcuffed to a chair and I felt like a balloon that had suddenly been pricked. I started to quiver. My eyes watered. I thought, what really happened here? My God, what happened? Until then, we'd been reacting. We hadn't time to think about it. We were more lucky than good. He could have blown anybody away."

The investigation and the trial

Once George Banks was in the custody, the detectives started talking with him in order to discover what exactly happened and why he snapped. He immediately told them that he would have committed suicide in the empty house if he knew that his children were dead. Even though he didn't want to give any details about the killings, he didn't deny that he was the perpetrator.

Banks didn't provide the investigators with plenty of details but they did have his mother's confirmation that he did, in fact, confess to her. There was no doubt that George Banks murdered his girlfriends and their children. However, his psychosis started to show at this point and Banks started talking about the conspiracy. Banks believed that the police officers were involved in murdering his wounded children.

Banks' trial was scheduled for 6th of October 1982 and he was transferred to Luzerne County Prison. He was calm and collected for the first couple of days in the lockup but he quickly started threatening the guards and even told them that he would commit suicide in his cell. He was put on round the clock watch and the guards didn't let him out of their sight.

The defense called Dr. Anthony Turchetti who conducted various examinations in order to determine if George Banks was coherent and that he understood the charges. Dr. Turchetti told them that Banks was not insane and that he could go through the trial. Banks didn't want to be tried in his hometown of Wilkes-Barre but the judge denied his plea. Instead, he made sure that the jury was selected from Pittsburgh, Pennsylvania because they didn't know the people involved in the case.

The trial began on 6th of June 1983. The prosecution was confident knowing that they have plenty of evidence to prove that George Banks was not insane and that he was of clear mind on the day of the murders. They had more than forty witnesses who were ready to talk about Banks' behavior prior to the killings. The evidence also included crime scene photos and his rifle.

On the other hand, George Banks was completely against the insanity plea. He claimed that he was innocent and that the police shot some of his wounded victims. However, his own attorneys did prepare the defense that would rely on his fragile state of mind, as well as the unusual lifestyle he led. After all, he has several girlfriends living with him at the time and the settings did remind the authorities of a cult-like place.

The trial was opened with the statement from Dr. Spodak, a psychiatrist who told the jury about the mental state of George Banks. He said that Banks was paranoid and suicidal. Banks would often talk about being a victim of a conspiracy and that the entire township was against him. The prosecution asked Dr. Spodak about his evaluation of the accused and is it possible that George Banks was faking the insanity. Dr. Spodak told them that he was certain Banks did believe in everything he said and that he was clearly delusional.

George Banks wanted to take the stand and tell the court his side of the story. His attorneys were against this because it would appear that he was not mentally ill and that his testimony would endanger their whole case. However, stopping Banks was almost impossible.

Once he got to the stand, Banks started rambling without any clear timeline of the events. He would jump from one killing to another without providing enough information to the courtroom. His demeanor was also odd because he simply couldn't sit still. He then dove into the conspiracy claims, saying that the police was out to get him because he has a mixed background and once again repeated the story that the law enforcement killed the remaining members of his family who were still alive after he shot them.

The defense tried salvaging their case by inviting Banks' mother and advisor to the stand. They were supposed to confirm that Banks suffered from a mental illness. However, the jury was already in shock after George's testimony and appeared completely uninterested in anything they had to say. It was time for the prosecution's side of the story.

They called James Olsen, who was one of the survivors from Schoolhouse Lane murders. He fully recovered and was fit to testify. Olsen told the courtroom that George Banks was the man who shot him and drove away, leaving him to die in front of his home. The prosecution then called the detectives who arrived at the crime scene at Schoolhouse Lane and they described everything they saw inside Banks' home. Their testimony had plenty of visuals because they also showed the crime scene photos.

The closing statements were delivered on 21st of June 1983. The defense attorneys once again repeated that Banks' mental health was questionable and that he was going through a lot of stress at the time when the murders were committed. They pointed out the custody battle and the loss of his job as a prison guard.

The prosecution pointed out Banks' criminal past and that he was prone to violence. They claimed that Banks knew exactly what he was doing on the day of the shootings and that he shouldn't have been out of the prison at all.

The judge talked to the jury for almost half an hour, giving them the last instructions before they exit the courtroom and start the deliberation. It didn't take them a long time to find George Banks guilty on all charges. Not a single member of the jury believed that Banks was insane or mentally unstable so they made their decision quickly.

The sentencing was delivered on 22nd of June. The jury returned to the courtroom after five and a half hours. The foreman stepped up and delivered the sentence. George Banks was found guilty on all charges and the jury recommended the death penalty. Banks stood calmly by his seat and his only comment was to the juror who was clearly distressed. He told her: "It's not your fault, ma'am. You were lied to. A two-hour exhumation would clear me."

George Banks was driven straight to Huntingdon maximum security prison after the sentencing. He stayed there until 1985. His attorneys were trying to overturn the conviction in front of the US Supreme Court but once their case was dismissed, Banks was transferred to State Correctional Institute at Graterford where he was locked up back in the 1960s.

The aftermath

George Banks continued his fight from the prison. His attorneys did their best to get him an appeal but the US Supreme Court turned it down every single time. The defense was set on proving that George Banks was mentally ill and that he shouldn't have been on trial in the first place. Banks have been placed on the list for execution twice since the imprisonment but the death penalty was delayed both times.

The reason behind the canceling of the executions was due to the fact that George Banks was indeed mentally ill. His paranoid schizophrenia took a toll on his mind and delivering the death penalty to someone who is not even aware of his surroundings simply doesn't feel right. Banks tried to commit suicide while incarcerated at least a couple of times so it is clear that he is not afraid to die.

Now, more than three decades after the murders, George Banks still stands behind his convictions that he murdered his children because he wanted to spare them the horrors of being mixed race. It appears that he really believed in the upcoming race wars. He continues to blame the law enforcement for shooting the children who survived the killing spree.

The residents of the Greater Wyoming Valley still remember that day in September of 1982 when the entire area was fearing the deranged shooter who was on the loose. It is one of the most well-known crimes in the area and a larger tragedy was prevented because the police reacted quickly. George Banks was very ill and he probably would have continued his killing spree, making this tragedy even bigger.